# Kira Muratova

**KINOfiles Filmmakers' Companions**
General Editor: Richard Taylor

Written for cineastes and students alike, and building on the achievements of the KINOfiles Film Companions, the KINOfiles Filmmakers' Companions are readable, authoritative, illustrated companion handbooks to the most important and interesting people who have participated in Russian cinema from its beginnings to the present. Each KINOfile examines the career of one filmmaker, or group of filmmakers, in the context of both Russian and world cinema. KINOfiles also include studies of people who have been active in the cinemas of the other countries that once formed part of the Soviet Union, as well as of émigré filmmakers working in the Russian tradition.

KINOfiles form a part of KINO: The Russian Cinema Series.

Filmmakers' Companions:

Film Companions:

# Contents

# Illustrations

# Acknowledgements

This book could not have been written without the generous help of Elena M. Vasilieva of Moscow, and without the gracious cooperation of Kira Muratova herself. I am thankful for the help generously provided to me by the Olexandr Dovzhenko National Centre in Kiev, its Director of Research, Sergei Trimbach, and the entire staff, including the General Director, Volodymir Mandryka, and the Librarian, Petro Jarovenko. Vira Komisarenko of the Olexandr Dovzhenko Museum helped with translations from Ukrainian to Russian. I thank Alla Verlotsky for helping to arrange my research trip to Kiev. Professors Katerina Clark, Vida Johnson and Josephine Woll, and my husband William Taubman, read and commented on the manuscript at various stages. Marina Madorskaya read and commented on several chapters.

Two anonymous readers provided extremely helpful suggestions, and finally, Richard Taylor provided both encouragement and careful reading throughout.

I thank Tatiana Babyonysheva, Inna Babyonysheva, Viktoria Schweitzer, Maya Turovskaya and Marina Goldovskaya for sharing with me their vast knowledge of Russian culture and cinema. The late Leonid Gurevich helped me begin this project by providing an introduction to Elena Vasilieva. I thank Aleksandra Sviridova for research assistance and advice, Ksenya Kiebuzinski, Archivist/Bibliographer of the Harvard Ukrainian Research Institute, for research assistance and xeroxing, Alla Karasova and present and past Amherst students Constantin Rusanov and Irina Ivanova for translations from Ukrainian to Russian, and Amherst students Jaime Atteniese, Christina Schutz, Nicholas White and Tarja Martikainen for research assistance. The staff of the Frost Library at Amherst College provided peerless reference and inter-library loan assistance.

The project was funded with an Amherst College Faculty Research award.

# 1. Odessa's Uncompromising Eccentric

I always knew that my films would some day see the light of day. I just didn't believe that I'd live to see it.

Kira Muratova, 1986[1]

Muratova's biography helps explain her fierce independence and stubborn insistence on making films her own way. Her mother was Romanian, her father Russian. Both were dedicated communists and professional Revolutionaries. Kira Georgievna Korotkova was born on 5 November 1934 in Soroki, Bessarabia, which was then part of Romania but is now in Moldova. When Bessarabia was ceded to the Soviets as part of the Molotov–Ribbentrop pact, her parents repatriated to the USSR. During the war her father parachuted into occupied Bessarabia to organise the resistance, but he was handed over to the Germans and executed.[2] After the war Kira and her mother, Natalia, returned to Romania, where she studied in a Russian-language school for the children of Soviet officers. After the school closed she finished the last three years of her studies in a Romanian school. 'This produced more than a bit of confusion in my head. My first language, my love of country, was Russian and Russia, and when I later returned to the Soviet Union I knew that I wanted to stay there.'[3] Natalia, a gynaecologist by training, became a high official in the socialist government of post-war Romania.[4] She served as a member of the committee that approved foreign films, taking Kira along with her to screenings. This gave Muratova extensive exposure to contemporary West European cinema, which was unavailable to contemporaries in the USSR.[5] She retained her Romanian citizenship until the early 1970s, after her mother's death, though her status as a foreigner complicated her travels within the USSR.

In 1952 Muratova returned to Moscow to study at the literature faculty of Moscow State University, but transferred after a year to VGIK, the All-Union – now All-Russian – Institute of Cinematography, where she studied with Sergei Gerasimov and graduated in 1959.[6] She remains devoted to her teacher: 'Gerasimov taught me to listen to human intonation, to notice how people talk, and to love that.'[7] The listening was particularly important; it is reflected in the unconventional relation of dialogue and soundtrack to image in Muratova's films. Though he is usually remembered as the director of Soviet classics such as *Komsomolsk* [1937] or *Quiet Flows the Don* [Tikhii Don, 1958], Gerasimov began his career in the 1920s in Leningrad as an actor with the neo-expressionist FEKS (Factory of the Eccentric Actor), a group led by Grigori Kozintsev and Leonid Trauberg. The Soviet film encyclopaedia characterised him as 'an actor of predominantly grotesque *emploi*'.[8] That taste for the grotesque and the eccentric lives on in Muratova's films. Gerasimov passed on the heritage of the early Soviet avant-garde to a director who used its discoveries and frequently paid it homage in her own work. Those who knew Muratova in her student days at VGIK recall that she stood out from the other girls, not only in the stylishness of her haircut and dress but also in her more Western independence of mind and bearing.[9] Admission to VGIK was very competitive, but eased by parental achievements or citizenship in a fraternal socialist state: Muratova, daughter of a fallen Soviet war hero and a Romanian communist official, would have been given preference on both counts.

While at VGIK she married her fellow student Alexander Muratov, son of a Ukrainian writer. Kira Korotkova is credited as the co-screenwriter for a three-reel short, *Spring Rain* [Vesennii dozhd', 1958], which he directed as a term project, in response to the Komsomol's call for help in its campaign against alcoholism. Kolia (beloved Russian actor Oleg Tabakov, in his first screen role) and Katia are young workers whose budding love affair runs into trouble when he shows up for a date with a bottle of vodka. The movie is professionally made, with pardonable borrowings from Kalatozov's *The Cranes are Flying* [Letiat zhuravli, 1957]: a flock of birds rises as the young couple walk down a deserted street; they conduct tender farewells as she climbs a circular staircase to her apartment. The couple co-directed a short diploma film, *By the Steep Ravine* [U krutogo iara, 1961], for which Muratova wrote the screenplay, based on a story by nature writer Gavriil Troepolsky. Troepolsky's hero, Senia Troshin, is a collective farm worker whose first love is hunting. A pair of wolves have been decimating the local flocks; he tracks them to their lair and kills them, using as bait one of their cubs, which he later adopts. Senia loves nature: not only does he adopt the cub but he protects a lost baby rabbit, releasing it in a spot where it will be safe from hawks. According to Muratov, they changed the ending in order to alter the film's moral message:

'Senia didn't hunt the wolves because he wanted to kill them for the benefit of the collective farm, but because his fellow workers badgered him about his love of nature. The wolf hunt was an excuse to spend an entire month in the forest, rather than in the fields.'[10] Muratova's deep attachment to animals was already evident in this early film.

After graduation the couple was invited to work at the Odessa Studio, which had undergone a renaissance during the Khrushchev 'Thaw' with the arrival of talented directors such as Marlen Khutsiev. They were assigned a screenplay about the economic problems of a collective farm. *Our Honest Bread* [Nash chestnyi khleb, 1964], Muratova recalled, was 'a strong social critique that pointed a finger at responsible Party leaders who meddle in agriculture when they know nothing about it, while the competent chairman of the kolkhoz had to submit to their directives'.[11] The issue was particularly delicate in 1964, the year in which Nikita Khrushchev, accused of just such meddling, was removed from office. *Our Honest Bread* was attacked by the very bureaucracy it dared to criticise.[12] The film's hero, collective farm chairman Makar Zadorozhny, is an older man wise in the ways of the land and of human nature, suspicious of bureaucrats and their machinations to fulfil arbitrary plans. But, in his absence, his son Alexander agrees to accept defective milking machines from a local factory in exchange for additional deliveries of fodder – the corrupt regional Party secretary is in cahoots with the factory director. An unusually frank romantic sub-plot concerns Alexander and the beautiful milkmaid Katia, who is forced to abort his baby when he abandons her and the village.

The finished film, though not nearly as innovative as Muratova's solo films, still contained excellent acting and imaginative cinematography, such as a striking shot of the shadows of mourners walking their bicycles in a funeral procession (to ride back the long way from the graveyard). But it was too pessimistic for the Kiev authorities, who demanded numerous changes. Muratov re-shot two scenes over his wife's objections. Muratova prefers to begin her creative biography with her first solo film, *Brief Encounters* [Korotkie vstrechi, 1967]: 'In *Our Honest Bread* I consider I was still a student. I still didn't understand anything about editing, and in general, together we basically argued. We had constant "folklore" compromises: we'll do this the way you want, and that the way I want. I didn't consider myself the real author of that film.' But several characters from the village appeared in her later films: 'I have a tendency to attract non-professionals, with whom I fall in love because they are amusing and unique.'[13] After *Our Honest Bread* the couple went their separate ways as directors, and soon their marriage dissolved as well. He left to work at the Dovzhenko Studio in Kiev; Muratova remained in Odessa with their daughter, Marianna.

Muratova's first two solo films, which contemporary viewers still find most accessible, were treated most harshly by the Soviet authorities, though there is little explicitly political in either. *Brief Encounters* was given the lowest-category release and shown largely in film clubs, often by Muratova herself, who toured the country with one of the few prints. *The Long Farewell* [Dolgie provody, 1971, released 1987] was banned entirely, despite the active support and intervention of Gerasimov. She was 'disqualified' (downgraded to a lower professional category), which effectively denied her the right to work independently as a director. Muratova demanded she be given other work at the studio, and was shown a list of vacancies, which began with cleaning lady and gardener's assistant. The first two suited her: 'I prefer physical labour to needless paper shuffling.' But it was 'awkward' for a director to work as a cleaning lady, so she was given various other jobs, including directing the studio museum and library and writing screenplays to order.[14] In 1978 she was allowed to make *Getting to Know the Big, Wide World* at the Lenfilm Studio, but the film's aesthetic displeased the authorities. The Odessa Studio demanded so many cuts to *Among the Grey Stones* [Sredi serykh kamnei, 1983] that she removed her name from the credits. Asked about those difficult years, Muratova was characteristically philosophical: 'I simply continued to live.' Of the bureaucrats who censored or mutilated her films:

> It's a kind of homage, isn't it? [...] By nature I am a very happy person. But I have a pessimistic vision of things... My films are not polemics. There's not a shadow of radical critique of ideology or politics. [...] Every time, they would say to me, "As a whole, it won't work. There are allusions, excesses, associations of ideas." Nothing concrete. But in fact, they wanted you to avoid making the audience think or grow sad.[15]

The 1970s were a difficult decade of cultural stagnation, when the Brezhnev regime suppressed artistic originality and political dissent. Aleksander Solzhenitsyn was exiled abroad, human rights activist Andrei Sakharov persecuted. Muratova's idol, director Sergei Paradjanov, was imprisoned from 1973 to 1977 on charges of homosexuality. The artistic and literary intelligentsia supported Paradjanov and eventually got him released, though only the bravest dared show their support by writing to him in the labour camp. Muratova wrote to him pessimistically about the mood of the intelligentsia. 'It's a shame we are so pitiful and weak. And cowardly. We take everything as a matter of course and keep waiting for someone to do something, we keep blaming someone for something, but just keep living our lives, as if nothing at all had happened. [...] Slavery has settled into my soul once and for all.'[16]

In the late 1980s, when her early films were brought off the shelf, two young Russian film critics compared Muratova to Alexei German and characterised their aesthetic as 'the striving to represent life in the forms of life itself... The spectator has the illusion that the director is not interfering at all with the train of action, that life on the screen is "allowed" to exist and flow according to its own logic, its own laws.'[17] By the time they wrote, Muratova's style had already evolved through the poetic realism of *Getting to Know the Big, Wide World* into the surrealism and hyper-realism of *Among the Grey Stones* and *A Change of Fate* [Peremena uchasti, 1987]. She still based her aesthetic on the *realia* of everyday life, but the events that take place, and the authorial stance towards them, are far from 'the illusion that life on the screen is allowed to exist and flow according to its own logic' – rather, they flow according to life's *illogic*.

Muratova's aesthetic has evolved with each new film, but she has always been *sui generis*, never a member of an identifiable school or movement.[18] In part, this is because of her status as an outsider in Soviet society. When asked if she had 'the impression that in the mid-1960s films like Shepitko's *Heat*, Tarkovsky's *Ivan's Childhood*, Ioseliani's *Falling Leaves*, Paradjanov's *Shadows of Forgotten Ancestors*, and Konchalovsky's *First Teacher* marked the emergence of a generation and a new cinema,' she replied: 'Certainly I watched those films. But I never sensed the existence of a movement. [...] Let's not forget that I came to the USSR from Romania... I was not like those who lived here for a long time, seeing all the defects and the period when it changed... I have a different biography.'[19] Paradjanov, though an Armenian raised in Tbilisi, became – like Muratova – a 'Ukrainian' film-maker who made his early films at the Dovzhenko Studio. *Shadows of Forgotten Ancestors* [Teni zabytykh predkov, 1965] and *The Colour of Pomegranates* [Tsvet granata, 1969] were trailblazing in their use of colour and camera motion, and for their move away from an emphasis on a legible narrative. Paradjanov's example was important in giving Muratova the impetus for visual experimentation and what she called 'ornamentalism' (*dekorativnost'*), beginning with her first colour film, *Getting to Know the Big, Wide World*.

In May 1986 the new, reformist leadership of the Union of Soviet Film-makers established a 'Conflicts Commission', designed to bring about the release of films that had been forbidden, cut or given extremely limited release over the previous thirty years. Among the first films brought off the shelf were *Brief Encounters* and *The Long Farewell*, censored for their 'incompatibility with the aesthetic canons of Socialist Realism' and their director's 'evident political unreliability'.[20] Their belated release, and the simultaneous discovery of their nearly unknown director, produced a mild sensation both at home and abroad. *The Long Farewell* won the FIPRESCI award at the 1987 Locarno Festival, where Muratova served on the jury, and the Special Prize at the All-Union Film Festival in 1988. A retrospective of Muratova's films was shown at the Festival of Women's Films in Créteil, France, in March

1988. Critics were amazed that the early films had not aged despite nearly two decades on the shelf. Their delayed release probably increased the positive response: stylistically and ideologically far ahead of their time in the 1960s and early 1970s, they seemed fresh and original, even timely, when they finally reached audiences in the late 1980s. Muratova was not only a 'suppressed director' but also a woman director who made woman-centred films. Reviews of the two films and interviews with Muratova began to appear in foreign, particularly French, cinema journals. She quickly became a cult figure, revered by lovers of serious Russian film, admired for her brilliant and totally idiosyncratic approach to film-making. She became a living classic by breaking all the classic rules. Like all great artists, she constantly pushed ahead of her audience, so that each new film provoked controversy and criticism as well as praise.

The title of *A Change of Fate*, Muratova's first Gorbachev-era film, was seen by many as symbolic and self-referential, though Muratova insists it was merely a chance coincidence. Offered the opportunity to film anything she wanted, she proposed two projects: the contemporary one which became *Asthenic Syndrome*, and an adaptation of Somerset Maugham's story 'The Letter'. The studio chose the Maugham, which became *A Change of Fate*. The title was a legal term used in defending murderers whose crimes seemed totally chance and out of character.[21] Twenty years after *Brief Encounters*, Muratova finally received long-denied recognition; in fact, she was made something of a poster child for perestroika. Characteristically clear-eyed and sardonic, she recalled her own change of fate.

> Yesterday they had said to me, 'Idiot, cross-eyed fool, get out of here!' Suddenly they said, 'You're a genius! Everything that you've done is wonderful!' Black became white, and it was, 'Come on, film, as quickly as possible, whatever you want.' [...] They started to make use of me for their own profit: 'Look how bad it was for Muratova, and how good it's become for her. So anyone who thinks things are still bad can just shut up.'[22]

In June 1988 Muratova was invited to London with fellow directors Alexander Sokurov and Andrei Smirnov by the National Film Theatre for a festival of newly unshelved Soviet films. She was outspoken about the recent changes in the possibilities of Soviet cinema.

> I don't expect anything and so rejoice in whatever comes…For so long I was pushed aside, denied completely, treated as someone of absolutely no worth and even less importance, whereas *now* I am being pushed forward, promoted, praised. Egotistically, I'm very ready to comply, but I'm also aware that I am being used – exploited![23]

Back in Odessa after being lionised in the West, Muratova began filming her masterpiece, the apocalyptic *Asthenic Syndrome* [Astenicheskii sindrom,

1989, released 1990], which won a Silver Bear at the 1990 Berlin Film Festival. One wonders what influence her foreign journeys had on the film. A pessimism about humanity in general? Perhaps her trips to Paris and London intensified her sense of the aesthetic ugliness of Soviet everyday life? *Asthenic Syndrome* is one of the most important films of the late Soviet period, comparable in the weight of its message to Georgian director Tengiz Abuladze's *Repentance* [Pokaianie, 1984, released 1986]. Abuladze's film confronted the psychological legacy of Stalinism. Its belated release in 1986 convinced Russians that Gorbachev was serious about his policy of glasnost, about opening up for investigation previously forbidden questions of Soviet history and society. While *Repentance* signalled the beginning of the perestroika era, *Asthenic Syndrome* foretold its end in the internal collapse of Soviet society.

1. Muratova at work

Muratova continues to make Russian-language films while living in what Russians call the 'near abroad'. After the break-up of the USSR she found herself a citizen of an impoverished Ukraine – a situation that has complicated the funding and circulation of her films in both the Russian and world markets. Nevertheless, since 1991 she has completed and released six feature-length films and one short film – more than the six full-length films she managed to make in the entire thirty-nine years of her career as a Soviet director: *The Sentimental Policeman* [Chuvstvitel'nyi militsioner, 1992], *Enthusiasms* [Uvlechen'ia, 1994], *Three Stories* [Tri istorii, 1997], *Letter to America* [Pis'mo v Ameriku, 1999], *Minor People* [Vtorostepennye liudi, 2001], *Chekhov's Motifs* [Chekhovskie motivy, 2002] and *The Tuner* [Nastroishchik, 2004]. Her post-Soviet films have been met by a range of responses, from the ecstatic to the bewildered. Post-Soviet audiences at first had little interest in Russian films at all, even less in films that challenged them aesthetically and thematically. Nevertheless, Russian and Ukrainian film critics continue to respect her as one of their few remaining world-class film-makers. She won the Nika (Russia's Oscar) for best film and director in 1994, and special prizes at the Kinotavr Festival in Sochi in 1992, 1994 and 1997. *Chekhov's Motifs* won the Film Critics' Award at the 2002 Moscow Film Festival. Muratova was awarded the first Andrzej Wajda Freedom Prize at the 50th annual Berlin Film Festival in 2000. The prize was presented by Wajda himself, 'in tribute to her lifetime of work in the cinema and her commitment to truth during the Soviet era'.

Though Muratova's films seem disparate at first glance, there are common threads. Thematically, the first six films can be arranged according to the dichotomy proposed by that great theorist of Russian culture, Woody Allen: the first three are about love, the second three about death. The two great themes continue to alternate, and occasionally combine, in her post-Soviet films: love (*The Sentimental Policeman*), love and death (*Enthusiasms*), death (*Three Stories, Minor People*) and finally, again, love (*Chekhov's Motifs*). The key phrase 'no one loves anyone' ('*nikto nikogo ne liubit*') appears in several of her films in various contexts and intonations. Rather than an assertion, it is rather a proposition she presents for examination, in the secret hope that it will be proven wrong.

Like most Russian women film-makers and writers of her generation, Muratova was initially uncomfortable with the terms 'feminism' and 'women's film'. Nevertheless, part of her uniqueness as an artist lies in qualities attributable to her woman's eye and ear, and to her intimate knowledge of women's lives. Her films are distinguished by their particularly penetrating, never idealising, and often merciless gaze at her female characters, and by her keen ear for the 'heteroglossia' of Russian, including various forms of female language often heard on the street, the workplace or in the home, but seldom in Soviet film or literature. Immediately after finishing *Asthenic Syndrome* Muratova travelled to the United States, in the autumn of 1989, with German and Sokurov, and visited Yale University, where I first met her. She spoke of her emotional exhaustion after *Asthenic Syndrome*, akin to that of its characters. She chose to show *Getting to Know the Big, Wide World*, not an easy film to understand for an audience unfamiliar with the traditions of Socialist Realism.

The following day Muratova was invited to a seminar on feminist theory. The students had watched her film and prepared to discuss it with her. I was recruited as a translator. As we walked to the seminar, she enquired, 'What, exactly, is feminist theory?' (something of which, in 1989, even the most sophisticated in the Russian intelligentsia were largely ignorant). I began to explain that there were different sorts of feminist theory: Marxist-feminist, Freudian-feminist, etc.; she looked apprehensive. But, after a long and lively exchange with the predominantly female students, she concluded with a comment intended as a compliment. As I prepared to translate it, however, my heart sank, anticipating their reaction. 'You know, I think that, if I hadn't found my *métier* in art, I too might have become a feminist.' Her views on the existence of 'women's film', however, were beginning to change. In 1990 she declared, 'I used to think that the division into male and female cinema was not simply artificial or wrong, but even stupid. But [in 1988] I attended the International Festival of Women Directors [in Créteil], and I found much of interest to me. Never at any another festival had I seen so many interesting films in all possible genres.'[24] Muratova claimed she often discouraged woman film-makers who asked her for advice. 'The life of a film-maker is so difficult in my country that if you have to ask or feel you need someone else's approval, you shouldn't even try. You must be so determined that nothing will stop you.'[25]

The same few names recur when she is asked to name those whose work influenced her.

> Charlie Chaplin and Fellini...they are universal teachers. Writers? Not Chekhov, to whom they're always linking me...Tolstoy represents for me something eternal, eternally recurring. And also as a teacher of structure. In other things I'm rather omnivorous...I love the brilliant director Sergei Paradjanov. I consider him my teacher...He had a great influence on me...And also Flaherty, his film *Louisiana Story*. There's a shot there with a boy and a little animal, the boy tosses him out of the boat several times, and it keeps crawling back again and again. I could watch that shot, with that boy and the animal, endlessly.[26]

The black humour of Chaplin and Fellini, Tolstoy's understanding of the psychological meaning of the most minute human actions, Paradjanov's love of colour and sheer beauty in cinema, and his courage to go beyond 'mere narrative' – all are essential characteristics of Muratova's work. The repetition she admired in Flaherty is also significant: it is a favourite device in almost all her films. So is her attraction to the raccoon and the boy: animals and children occupy an important place in her work. Elsewhere, she remarked: 'I always prefer a bad American film to a good French film ... What I like in American cinema is its sporting side, its richness, its vitality ... The French cinema in general – there are exceptions – lacks air. It makes me think of a patient who is ready to die and who appreciates everything that is still alive.'[27] Recently she named Godard and Pasolini as her current favourites, but added, 'I've fallen out of love with Bergman'. And not Tarkovsky: 'I don't like his missionary manner and his meditations on sacrifice, predestination: "Oh, how I am suffering. None of you knows how to suffer as I do."'[28] Asked in 1987 whom she liked in Soviet film she replied, 'Today, Paradjanov. In the past, Eisenstein, particularly *Ivan the Terrible*.'[29]

How does she feel about the fact that her films have often been met with misunderstanding and hostility?

> I don't like conversations about the 'courage of the artist', about 'faithfulness to oneself'. How can you not be faithful to yourself? [...] I agree with Helvetius, who says that man is ruled by a desire for pleasure. But everyone's pleasure is different. Directing, with all the complications that go along with it, is what gives me pleasure. Otherwise, why would I do it? Perhaps it's only five minutes of happiness, but for their sake it's worth suffering through everything.[30]

Andrei Plakhov, a staunch defender of Muratova's work and chair of the Conflicts Commission that unshelved her first two films, dubbed Muratova 'the *enfant terrible* of Soviet cinema' and 'a provincial anarchist'.[31] An anarchist in her relation to accepted artistic rules, she is 'provincial' by virtue of her forty years in Odessa. Except for her student years in the 1950s and early 1960s, Muratova has spent very little time in Moscow, the centre of the Russian film industry. She shot most of her films in Odessa, a multi-ethnic 'city state' with its own rich cultural history, cityscape and distinctive dialect. Her Romanian childhood and Odessa adulthood have doubly distanced her from what Russians call 'the kino-process'. Her 'marginality' is an essential element of her aesthetic and her world-view.

# 2. 'Provincial Melodramas'

Kira Muratova's world is essentially simple, regardless of the seeming complexity of her films. It is simple because at its foundation lie precise, very familiar, but sometimes overlooked, human values.

Irina Shilova[1]

Muratova called her first two films 'provincial melodramas', but her meaning is tinged with irony. For neither is characterised by melodrama's 'strong plot, contrasting opposition of good and evil, well-defined typecasting of the characters';[2] rather, the opposite. Both films explore the emotions of a mature single woman – emotions that she does not herself fully understand. Plot events are subtle rather than dramatic; the 'crisis' is in the characters' recognition of reality, not a change in that reality itself. They are, however, definitely provincial in their setting: both were shot in Odessa and highlight recognisable features of that legendary city's life – its water shortages, port, and architecture, as well as the distinctive south Russian dialect of her non-professional actors.

The mirror-image titles emphasise the links between the two films and their common concern with human connection: *Brief Encounters*, *The Long Farewell*. Valentina, the city government bureaucrat of *Brief Encounters*, and Evgeniia, the technical translator of *The Long Farewell*, are well-educated women past the first blush of youth. Each is genuinely devoted to her responsible job, but the men in their lives want no part of their settled existence. Valentina's lover, the footloose geologist Maxim, lives with her in the brief intervals between his expeditions. Evgeniia's adolescent son Sasha wants to leave the single room he has shared all his life with his divorced mother to live with his father, whose life on archaeological expeditions promises a freedom similar to Maxim's. Neither Valentina nor Evgeniia can cope with separation, nor admit how upsetting it really is to her. Each hides her emotions behind stereotyped attitudes and clichéd language. Muratova defamiliarises these emotions so that her audience, in tandem with her heroines, comes to a fresh realisation of their power. After the appearance of *Asthenic Syndrome*, Plakhov connected the personal predicament of Muratova's early heroines with larger social issues.

> Now it has finally become clear what Muratova had in mind (it seems the censors were among the first to understand this) in her early films, when she filled them full of female languor and agitation. The capricious, high-strung emotions came not from loneliness, from the absence of a concrete man... but from the suspicion that 'man' in general no longer exists in this world, that he has become a myth, like Vysotsky's hero from *Brief Encounters*, like Vysotsky himself.[3]

Shilova agrees. 'A strange migration rules the world. The five films of Kira Muratova are five acts in the drama of an individual. But they are also five acts in the global drama of total assault on humanity by civilization.'[4]

The aesthetic of these two films is distinct from that of the rest of Muratova's work. Except for *Chekhov's Motifs* and the first part of *Asthenic Syndrome*, these are the only films she shot in black and white. Black and white, notes Josephine Woll, was one of several means used by Thaw film-makers who 'strove to satisfy the popular thirst for "verismo"'. Citing Shilova, she notes that 'paradoxically, although black-and-white film deprives the viewer of a central characteristic of objective reality, it affirms the veracity of what is on the screen'.[5] Muratova intensified that veracity with her extraordinarily sharp eye for the details of everyday domestic *realia*, of human speech and of gesture.

## *Brief Encounters* [1967]

The plot of *Brief Encounters* is simple, although the film's narrative is conveyed in a complex series of flashbacks. Nadia (Nina Ruslanova), a village girl working as a waitress in a roadside café, falls in love with the guitar-playing Maxim (Vladimir Vysotsky) and tracks down his address in the city. It turns out to be the apartment of Valentina (Kira Muratova), a member of the city soviet in charge of water and sewage. She assumes the girl at her door has been sent to work as a live-in housekeeper; Nadia, not revealing her friend-ship with Maxim, accepts the job. In his absence, Nadia studies Valentina, trying to understand her and her relationship with Maxim. The fact that the marriage is not officially registered complicates matters for both Nadia and the audience, though Valentina refers to him as her 'husband'. Muratova was intrigued by the conflict between Valentina's settled, domestic personality and Maxim's free spirit: Valentina nearly drives him away with her bossy behaviour and impatience with his absences. Yet Valentina is no ogre; Muratova plays her without idealisation, but sympathetically, as an attractive, believable human being who loves her work and genuinely tries to make people's lives better. On the eve of Maxim's return, Nadia silently acknowledges Valentina's priority by setting the table for their reunion dinner and slipping out of the door to return home.

*Brief Encounters* had a magical cast: Vysotsky, then twenty-nine, had acted in several mostly forgotten films, but was already well known as an underground bard. This was the first screen role for Ruslanova, then a second-year acting student of twenty-one. By the time the film was re-released twenty years later she was a major star, and Vysotsky, who died in 1980, had become a legend. But the casting did not go easily. To play Maxim, Muratova originally chose Stanislav Liubshin, who had starred in Khutsiev's *Lenin's Gate/I Am Twenty* [Zastava Il'icha, released as Mne dvadtsat' let, 1964]. But his role in the popular spy movie *Shield and Sword* [Shchit i mech, 1968] conflicted with her shooting schedule. Vysotsky, who had also auditioned for the role, graciously agreed to step in. The theatrical actress originally cast as Valentina seemed to work well in rehearsal. But when Muratova looked at the early rushes she realised that 'there was something in her that the screen revealed, and it destroyed her'.[6] There was neither time nor money in the budget to find a replacement. While casting the male lead, Muratova had played her role opposite a number of actors, and members of the crew proposed that she play it herself.[7]

Most of the other actors were non-professional. The old man in the café was a retired circus clown, and Nadia's gabby girlfriend Liuba, with her heavy south Russian accent, was a milkmaid Muratova met while filming *Our Honest Bread*. Muratova paid a lot of attention to secondary characters, 'perhaps because I get bored working with the same characters all the time. Whether I'm writing, rehearsing, or editing, I need variety.'[8] She attributed her fondness for non-professionals to the spirit of the times: 'It was fashionable, in conversation, to want to create a slice of life, to use the documentary form. But I was interested in the question simply cognitively: what is an actor, and how much of an actor is there in each person, and where is the boundary between actor and non-actor?'[9]

Vladimir Gulchenko has observed that the plot is less a love triangle than two parallel story lines that meet somewhere beyond the frame of the film.[10] In fact, this reflects the genesis of the screenplay, which Muratova wrote in collaboration with Leonid Zhukhovitsky. Her storyline came from Odessa's chronic water supply problems, and she wanted a central character who dealt with the issue. 'I was surprised both by the absence of water and by the indifference of the inhabitants to what was going on, the way they had gotten used to it.'[11] 'That was how the woman bureaucrat appeared, and then a romantic plot with some sort of lover, but she was so pedantic and official, and the lover had a free, gypsy-like character, like a cloud which she wanted to take over and shape, but he doesn't give in.'[12] The field geologist's escape from the political and social strictures of Soviet society was idealised by Thaw-era intellectuals – even the young Joseph Brodsky worked on one such expedition.

The Nadia/Maxim plot line came from Zhukhovitsky's short story, 'The House in the Steppe'. Nadia loves village life but is forced out into the world by forces beyond her control. In the Khrushchev era young men often remained in the cities after their compulsory military service, leaving the villages to old men and women and girls with no marriage prospects. Muratova's experience filming *Our Honest Bread* taught her the real truth of village life and inspired authentic dialogue, such as Valentina's conversation with a country lad who explains the real cost of raising hogs and producing sausage. The film retained elements of Zhukhovitsky's story, including Nadia's scheming boss Stepan, who tries to teach her to trade 'intelligently' – i.e. making a few kopeks off each transaction by short-weighting the sausage or leaving a bit of water in the bottom of the vodka glass. But Muratova's Nadia, in Ruslanova's interpretation, is a far more interesting character than Zhukhovitsky's skinny, pale-browed seventeen-year-old. She is a self-contained young woman with deep roots in her native village. In the finished film, the most interesting and fully developed

2. *Brief Encounters*: Nina Ruslanova, Vladimir Vysotsky

relationship is that between the two women, rather than between either of them and Maxim. Of his collaboration with Muratova, Zhukhovitsky recalls, 'My story was a man's story; it became clear that Kira wanted to make a woman's film'.[13]

Lev Anninsky argues that just below the surface of this chamber drama lies 'an abyss of social incomprehension'. Valentina, the urban intellectual, lives in a book-lined apartment with fine old furniture. Like the party she represents, she blithely assumes she is making people's lives better with her speeches and inspections. But she has no idea how unnecessary most of her 'administration' really is:

> Why, after all, should the kindly Valentina Ivanovna Sviridova, from her city apartment or even from her city soviet office, determine the price of sausage which is made in the village? [...] Why does she agree to urge young people to move to the countryside, when from that very countryside, right before her eyes, young people are fleeing, and she knows very well why?[14]

Zina, a young working-class woman, borrows books from Valentina's large library, and is teased at work about not getting married. 'Perhaps,' she complains plaintively to Valentina, 'it's because of you...I used to like the guys with pretty faces, but now I like the smart ones. I like them, but they don't like me.' ''Cause I'm not smart. They don't find me interesting.' Nadia, silently washing Valentina's windows, listens attentively. One defiant gesture expresses her passive resistance: she erases the speech Valentina is rehearsing from the tape recorder. 'That's all nonsense,' she mumbles when Valentina confronts her. 'You've got to love farming.'

In the film, Maxim is never seen in real time, only in the flashbacks of the two women who love him. The only contemporary review complained, 'When you look at the picture, you get the impression that the director, sitting at the editing table, simply rearranged individual pieces of film, without, essentially, justifying this rearrangement'.[15] The sixteen flashbacks take up nearly half the film and are its crucial structural element; were the story told sequentially, it would lose its narrative suspense. Muratova carefully signalled each flashback subtly but effectively, often with a fade to white or with music. Ten of them are from Nadia's point of view, but Muratova arranged them into groups of two or three, with brief real-time shots of a pensive Nadia in between. Valentina's flashbacks are fewer but longer, and psychologically deeper in probing the couple's contrasting characters.

*Brief Encounters* opens with a bravura tracking shot confined within the small space of Valentina's kitchen. She sits at the table in a bathrobe, surrounded by the dishes and pots of domesticity, but not engaged in housekeeping. For several seconds the only movement is a pencil, with which she beats time to a ticking clock. Finally, she speaks: 'Comrades...! Dear

Comrades…! Dear, Dear Comrades…!' Telling domestic details define Valentina's character. The unwashed dishes and solid, old-fashioned chair are not the usual mass-produced Soviet consumer goods but something finer, perhaps family heirlooms. Her educated pronunciation and the speech she is writing signal that she is a functionary of some sort. The camera centres on the table, with her open notebook against a contrasting still life of kitchen utensils, then tilts up, and for the first time we see the face of an attractive, vibrant woman in her late twenties or early thirties (Muratova was a youthful thirty-three at the time). 'But should I wash the dishes, or leave them… To wash or not to wash [*myt' ili ne myt'*], that is the question' – a playful parody of Hamlet's 'to be or not to be' (*byt' ili ne byt'* in Russian). Muratova counterpoints Valentina's playful natural language with the stilted Soviet rhetoric in which she is trying to write. The camera follows her as she paces back and forth, performing both parts of an imagined conversation – 'I'll leave the dishes, OK? You won't scold me? You will, yes? Well, scold on, to your heart's content… I don't give a damn!' – singing the final word, 'give a damn, give a damn' (*naplevat'*) to the familiar tune of Figaro's aria ('Non più andrai, farfallone amoroso') from *The Marriage of Figaro*. The shot finally ends with an extended focus on a pile of dirty, mismatched, though elegant dishes. In less than two minutes we have been charmed and engaged by a woman who can parody Shakespeare, Mozart and herself, while the tracking shot has conveyed her lack of enthusiasm about both domestic and Party tasks. Valentina's internal battle with officious Soviet-speak parallels that of her creator Muratova, who played the role with sympathy and gusto.

Valentina phones her superior to beg off the assignment, then gets into bed. Suddenly there is the sound of a breaking string; cut to a guitar hanging on the bedroom wall. This can only be a playful reference to the famous sound 'like a breaking string' in Chekhov's *The Cherry Orchard*, which dealt with change in the Russian countryside at an earlier historical moment. Pensively, Valentina turns the light on and off. As if in answer to this signal, the doorbell rings. The blinking light will be clearly visible in Nadia's final flashback at the end of the film as she approaches Valentina's house for the first time, the circular structure a brilliant directorial touch. Muratova's introduction of Nadia is unconventional: no expository shot of the door opening, simply an extreme close-up – with silence on the soundtrack – of a young woman in the doorway, head wrapped in a scarf in the village manner, with an expression of surprise and discomfort. Muratova challenges her audience, forcing them to figure out the situation for themselves. We are in Valentina's position; unaware of Nadia's love for Maxim, we are puzzled by the unexpected appearance of this moody, laconic country girl. Irina Izvolova has pointed out the unusual importance of the sense of touch in Muratova's films. 'The physicality of the world is not observed by the audience, but rather sensed by her characters.' This is how Nadia begins to explore Valentina's world: 'Nadia's hand slides along the wall, across the back of a chair, across the bed sheet. Slowly, like the hand of a blind person, it comprehends the texture of things.'[16] She wanders over to touch the guitar, evoking the first flashback to her infatuation with Maxim at the roadside café. Back in real time, the two women lie in their beds. Now it is Valentina's face that expresses longing, introducing a flashback to a romantic interlude on the veranda of her apartment. The spectator suddenly realises that Valentina's lover is the geologist we have just seen with Nadia. Subtle parallels link the two flash-backs: the porch/veranda locations, the birdsong on the soundtrack, the white blouses with dark patterns that the women are wearing. In a later flashback Muratova conveys the awkward fit of Valentina and Maxim's relationship by framing them off-centre in a bedroom mirror. In another she photographs them from the bottom of a pot, through boiling water in which still-swimming crayfish are cooking – a physically impossible shot.

Nadia sceptically follows Valentina as she inspects a new apartment building, refusing to approve it because the water system doesn't work. 'Why are you always in a whirl like this?' she asks. 'I love it,' Valentina replies. 'I love the fact that somehow everything around us will change.' But her more realistic

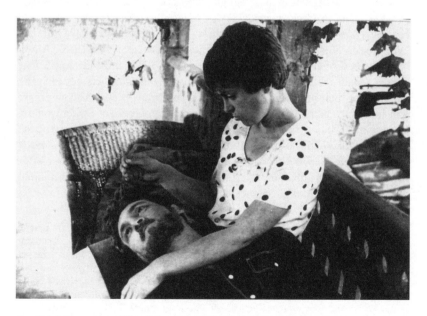

3. *Brief Encounters*: Kira Muratova, Vladimir Vysotsky

afterthought did not please the censors: 'But generally it only seems to me that something is changing. You look the next day, and it's back in the same place.' When a tape recorder is delivered to the astonished Valentina, she phones the store and discovers it had been ordered before the date of her last quarrel with Maxim, after which he left, threatening never to return. Nadia finds her in tears. Izvolova observes, 'Once again, in place of the real arrival of her beloved, Valentina Ivanovna receives another indirect proof of his existence in the form of a tape recording. And she ceases to be afraid of her feelings – she begins to sense the much greater danger of their absence.'[17] At this point Nadia, reversing their roles, takes charge and gets Valentina to bed. The ending of *Brief Encounters* is ambiguously open-ended. Nadia sets a festive table for two for Maxim's promised return, then pulls her suitcase from under the bed and puts on her boots. On her way out through the door she snatches one orange – a last taste of city life – from the table and exits, accompanied by Oleg Karavaichuk's upbeat dance-hall-style music, which has accompanied the more romantic moments of Valentina's flashbacks. Anninsky raves about the final shot: 'The absence of one orange slightly destroys the harmony of the composition – recalling the drama of the film.'[18]

*Brief Encounters* was only one of several films made in 1966–1967, at the very end of the Khrushchev-inspired Thaw, featuring capable, unmarried heroines, two of whom were single mothers. Larissa Shepitko's *Wings* [Kryl'ia, 1966], Andrei Konchalovsky's *The Story of Asya Kliachina, Who Loved but Didn't Marry* [Istoriia Asi Kliachinoi, kotoraia liubila, da ne vyshla zamuzh, 1966, released as *Asya's Happiness*, restored with original title 1988], Alexei Askoldov's *Commissar* [Komissar, 1967, released 1988] and Muratova's *Brief Encounters* all featured heroines who struggle with conflicts between the demands of their profession and those of love, family or – in the wider sense – of humanity, going far beyond the Stalin-era stereotypes of Soviet woman-hood: either Cinderella or all-capable Amazon. These films were among the first cinematic victims of the cultural crackdown under Brezhnev. *Commissar* and *Asya* were denied distribution entirely, while *Wings* and *Brief Encounters* received limited distribution.[19] According to Muratova, Goskino voiced moral objections to Valentina's romance with Maxim.

The times were then very naive. 'Why a love triangle with an important person and her responsible job at the centre? Why this immorality in a government official, why does she have a lover, where is her husband, why doesn't she get married, who's this geologist, some sort of suspicious character, why does he have some kind of girl?' They tried to figure out the place in the scenario where Maxim reaches out his hand to take back his jacket from Nadia: was he just taking his jacket, or did they embrace and go off into the bushes? 'If that's the case,' they said, 'we won't pass it.'[20]

Andrei Zorky tries to imagine the thinking of a 1967 film censor:

Who is this 'responsible official' whom we meet not in the thick of life or in her office, but in a messy apartment and, excuse me, in a nightgown? What kind of unsettled life is this, her familiarity with her servant, catching snacks in a cafe, as if there weren't a respectable, restricted-access office lunch room? What kind of a reprehensible, unregistered liaison of a high official with a bearded guitar-playing geologist? What's with all this shameless lovemaking? Those shameless crayfish with beer?

He praises Muratova's 'utter inability to depict life "as it should be", and not as it is... In [Valentina] we see perhaps the first moral portrait of a contemporary "professional woman" in our cinema, long before *I Want the Floor* [Proshu slova, 1976; Gleb Panfilov's film starring Inna Churikova].'[21] That portrait, enriched by Muratova's memories of her mother's official career, remains compelling to this day.

After *Brief Encounters* Muratova turned to a screenplay she had co-authored titled 'Watch Out for Your Dreams!' [*Vnimatel'no smotrite sny!*]. She was ready to begin filming when the project was aborted. She recalls, 'For me this screenplay was like a sickness – I was "ill" with it for three years and didn't want to do anything else.' The strange story, originally suggested to her by Khutsiev, echoes that of H.G. Wells' 'The Door in the Wall'.

A woman artist is oppressed by the fact that she has to earn her living with hack work, that she doesn't have time for 'pure art'. She dreams of how it would be if she weren't burdened by a house, a family, a mother, a child... Then she meets a handsome man who takes her in a car to a dacha and asks, 'Wouldn't you like to live here?' And there, in the situation of which she had dreamed, when nothing prevented her from working, she couldn't work. She goes home, ostensibly to fetch something she needs, and immediately fights with her mother, who tells her the child is missing... In panic, thinking the child is at the dacha, she tries to return there, but can't find it. Then there are various interpretations, she is studied by psychiatrists, and finally the child simply turns up in the courtyard of her apartment house, but being small, cannot say what happened to him.[22]

There are obvious parallels with her own situation as the Brezhnev-era 'stagnation' set in: a woman artist wants to work as she wishes, not do hack work; and she has family responsibilities that get in her way – a house, a mother, a child.

## *The Long Farewell* [1971]

Muratova contrived to make the first non-Soviet – not to be confused with anti-Soviet – films in the history of our cinema...They began the 'long farewell' of Soviet cinema.

Andrei Plakhov[23]

Many of Muratova's admirers, including this one, still consider *The Long Farewell* her best film. Critics are unanimous in praising it. With its boldly unconventional montage and relation of soundtrack to image, this is a much more radical film, cinematically, than *Brief Encounters*. During the sixteen years that *The Long Farewell* was withheld from release it was regularly shown to students at VGIK, in Moscow, where it influenced a whole new generation of Soviet film-makers. As late as 1998 an informal poll of VGIK students, by a large margin, rated it Muratova's most successful film.[24]

Divorcée Evgeniia Vasilevna, brilliantly acted by Zinaida Sharko, has spent fifteen years working at the same desk as a technical translator. She is equally stuck in the rut of her mothering role, refusing to acknowledge that her son Sasha has grown up, as in many ways she refuses to grow up herself. She cannot let go of him, even to begin a relationship with a sympathetic man (Yuri Kaiurov) who is interested in her. Muratova subjects her heroine to a steely-eyed, penetrating gaze that reveals her worst faults. But, like Valentina in *Brief Encounters*, Evgeniia is no caricature. Sharko makes her sufficiently sympathetic for us to cringe in embarrassment when she publicly nags Sasha to clean his nails, or bribes a postal worker to let her read his letters from his father, or creates a scene over seats at the office celebration.

Muratova's old friend Natalia Riazantseva had encountered unexpected obstacles with this seemingly benign coming-of-age scenario.[25] It was bought by the Mosfilm Studio's youth division, but the time was inauspicious – the autumn of 1968, just after the Soviet invasion of Czechoslovakia. The authorities were particularly sensitive to any hint of cultural dissidence, and films were being shelved in the increasing cultural crackdown. Veteran director Alexander Zarkhi gave Riazantseva's screenplay a strong recommendation: 'The theme of the parent/child relationship is treated in an interesting and somewhat unusual way ... The screenplay encourages youth to be kinder, more attentive, more humane.' Of Evgeniia Vasilevna he wrote, 'At first glance, she seems banal and unpleasant, but later we discover in her genuinely strong emotions towards her son, and a human depth'.[26] Screenwriter Mikhail Bleiman added: 'We have got too used to a film and a screenplay being "about" something. And we feel a bit at a loss when faced with a screenplay that is simply about life without foregrounding a "problem".' Nevertheless, the screenplay was rejected by the State Screenplay Editorial Board (GSRK).

Riazantseva made some changes, primarily in secondary characters, and the script was assigned to Vladimir Diachenko, who had already had bad luck with two other directing projects. Permission was again requested to begin filming, but Riazantseva was called in by Vladimir Baskakov, deputy chair of the USSR Council of Ministers Committee on Cinematography. She recalls that one member of his committee berated her, 'We won't allow you to set the intelligentsia against the people! It's not your smart-alec young boys who won the war, but the people!'[27] Baskakov fulminated in a letter of 12 May 1969: 'Why is the mother depicted this way? [...] She once made a mistake[!], she's an ordinary person, a humble, low-status worker. But she has raised a good son. Isn't that the essential thing? [...] To depict her this way is a ridiculous, arrogant "intelligentsia" position.' In her original version, Riazantseva's heroine was a typist, and her ex-husband an archaeologist. She gave Evgeniia a higher education, but it didn't help.

In desperation, Riazantseva proposed the screenplay to Muratova and the Odessa Studio. They even renamed the project 'To Be a Man' in an effort at camouflage. Bleiman again defended the film. 'There are problems that seem "trivial" but are nevertheless important... If Gorky was right when he said that art must encourage an emotional culture, a culture of feelings and conduct, then it is precisely this culture that Riazantseva's screenplay educates.' He cautioned, 'This screenplay has evidently been earmarked for Kira Muratova. I don't like her film all that much. But she's undoubtedly talented. And this screenplay is written with an eye to her potential and inclinations.' The conservative film scholar Rostislav Yurenev found the film not didactic enough: 'This script is written in the fashionable "contemporary" manner... there's no plot... The author allows [the spectator] the right to try to make sense of the stream of life and make his own ethical, moral, ideological conclusions, as if freed from the author's influence.' He predicted, 'You can make a film from Riazantseva's screenplay, but it will be a weak and boring film, in which our people and our times will look very depressing'. The film's prospects also looked depressing. But Muratova resorted to the influence of Gerasimov, who vouched for her and got the project approved 'at the highest level'. Production began in Odessa in the spring of 1970, but on 15 July the Cinema Committee of the Ukrainian SSR ordered it stopped because the director of the Odessa Studio had not sent them the script for approval: '"To Be a Man" has a number of important shortcomings, and in its current version cannot be the basis for production of a worthwhile film in ideological-artistic terms.'

But fate intervened. In August an epidemic of cholera quarantined the entire southern region of Russia, threatening to upset the sacred yearly 'plan' of the studio. The order to begin production was given on 5 November, and Muratova began filming mid-summer scenes in the late autumn. She had nearly finished the film when, on 2 March 1971, an ominous telegram from Boris Pavlenok himself, the head of Goskino, summoned Muratova to Moscow. After looking at the material she had shot the editorial board demanded major changes; the extra scenes that they had requested 'were filmed in an atmosphere of estrangement and psychological isolation of the heroes'. Their principal demand concerned the heroine, 'who still in several scenes is devoid of charm, sympathy for others, fully admirable character'. Sasha's inner world was 'lacking contacts with his peers and the external world'. Their eight demands, laid out in a letter of 24 March 1971, illustrate the bureaucrats' obsessive concern with elements that were less than cheerful and optimistic.

Among them: 'In the final scene at the celebration it should shown that people have a respectful attitude to Evgeniia Vasilevna.' 'Think about ways Evgeniia Vasilevna's sympathetic attitude towards others can be given concrete expression, perhaps in helping Tanya find a job.' (This accounts for the otherwise unmotivated episode in which Evgeniia does, indeed, try to find Sasha's shiftless friend Tanya a job.) 'Shorten the scene of Evgeniia Vasilevna's conversation with her boss, and also underline in the following episode the justice of her indignation that an outside translator has been invited.' 'Remove the drawn-out sections in several episodes (at the cemetery, with the dead seagull, at the stadium, the scene where Sasha composes verses).'

> Shorten the episode in the taxi … find a more precise place in the montage for the scene with the letter at the post office … Add scenes in which there would be room found for showing the bright and optimistic face of the contemporary city … Clarify a number of scenes (at the dacha, at work) where there is much bustling and milling around of faces on the screen, which creates the impression of meaninglessness and an excessive nervous tension of life.

Muratova acceded to some of these demands, but many other episodes, among the film's finest, remained seemingly untouched. She showed great courage and persistence to preserve her vision.

4.  *The Long Farewell*: Muratova directs Oleg Vladimirsky

The Long Farewell was finished in June and brought to Moscow on 6 July 1971, an official document accepting it was signed on 12 July, and it was offered to the All-Union Festival. But the final blow, Fomin recounts, citing the evidence of a former official of Goskino (who in 1991 still preferred to remain anonymous), was that the film became a pawn in a bureaucratic campaign being waged by F. Yermash, the new head of Goskino, who was looking for a pretext to speed a resolution by the Central Committee about the 'unsatisfactory situation in the film industry'. Muratova's film was a timely target. It was sent around to the dachas of high officials, 'as if foreseeing in advance that it would evoke scandal'. And it did. 'They didn't see any obvious sedition,' writes Fomin, 'but they were terribly unnerved by the film's form.' The Central Committee sent a threatening letter to the Ukrainian Central Committee: 'How could you allow such an outrage?' The film was banned, and the chair of the Ukranian Cinema Committee was fired. Yermash's Central Committee resolution was passed.

Muratova recalls the objections to the film: 'This is petty-bourgeois, this is shameful, this discredits... Nothing more! You mustn't film a cemetery, you mustn't film about death, it's impossible to have any scenes in a hospital, you can't use this word or that word.' But she was able, in retrospect, to appreciate the humour in the situation.

> The Party organizer of the temporary Party cell in our filming group turned out to be the make-up woman. She was called in and asked, 'How could you have taken part in such a decadent film? How did you allow this to happen?' She defended herself: 'I didn't know what they were filming, I was just doing the make-up, I didn't have any idea what sort of ideological diversion they had cooked up.'[28]

Alexandra Sviridova, working as a student intern on the filming of The Long Farewell, witnessed the scene at the studio when the film was banned. 'There was a screening and an open meeting at which the Party leader of the studio, hastily wiping away the tears that she had shed during the whole film, began to enumerate the failings that made it necessary to forbid it.'[29] The few existing copies of The Long Farewell were marked with white chalk on the canister 'Not to be given out'.

Muratova kept much of Riazantseva's dialogue and many of her major scenes, but shifted the focus to the mother, usually the forgotten figure – if not simply the villain – in the coming-of-age drama. The most memorable episodes, which provide the film's poetry and help us understand Evgeniia, emerged entirely from Muratova's imagination. Exploiting Odessa's resources, she transformed Riazantseva's 'visit to friends at a dacha' by making the location a nearly deserted *pension* by the sea, where the windswept autumn waves provide a background for Sasha's seething adolescent emotions. The hostess's daughter Masha (Tatiana Mychko), one year Sasha's senior, has been a childhood friend, but now he is all too aware of her womanly charms and painfully embarrassed in her presence. Muratova invented marvellous dream shots of Sasha kissing Masha's hair and a sequence in which their hands touch as they mutually stroke a dog. A shot of a dying seagull on the beach evokes an undefined Chekhovian nostalgia. She also invented the striking device of projecting slides against the white double door of the room shared by mother and son. Sasha, alone, views slides of paintings, perhaps from his father's archaeological digs. Evgeniia enters unexpectedly to dress for a theatre date, breaking into the image. Later, in a mirror-image scene, she is alone in the room, surreptitiously projecting slides Sasha's father has sent of their summer together in the Crimea. Images of father and son flash on the white door, broken this time by Sasha's entrance.

In *The Long Farewell*, Muratova was interested in exploring montage.[30] Three nearly identical takes of Sasha standing and turning to look out of the greenhouse window (hoping for escape), like three different variants in a poem, provide alternative possibilities as well as a change in rhythm. Izvolova observes:

> The shots in her films begin to exist autonomously from each other, like chance snapshots of reality taken at different times and places – they've been accidentally reshuffled and have completely lost the sequence of alternation of actions...She breaks down complex episodes into an infinite number of similar acts, but doesn't even stop at that, since even the simplest action in the shot is in turn divisible.[31]

In the cemetery sequence the freedom of Gennadi Kariuk's camera is striking; it looks almost everywhere except where we would expect – at Evgeniia's shoes, at the pattern of the fences that partially obscure our view of her and Sasha, at a pile of smouldering leaves. Evgeniia reminisces about her father, a man of traditional Russian patriarchal views. Judging by the rapid pace at which she recites her monologue and the boredom with which Sasha receives it, she has told this story many times before. In her narrative, as throughout the film, Evgeniia is playing (usually overplaying) the various roles assigned to her by social expectations – the dutiful daughter, the attractive, flirtatious woman (although clearly past her prime), the professional translator, and, above all, the devoted mother of her son. It is the genius of Sharko's acting that she can depict Evgeniia's overacting to the point at which we feel almost physically uncomfortable from embarrassment but yet have compassion, sympathy and even respect for her (as does her son). The soundtrack suddenly falls silent as she plants flowers she has bought; we literally hear a fly buzz as Muratova creates an evocative montage sequence of Evgeniia's face, the red star on her father's monument, his stern portrait etched on the gravestone, her hands watering the plants. Izvolova observes: 'The close-up of the shake of her hands is repeated several times in such a way that the rapid quivering of her fingers becomes like the trembling of wings. The shot doesn't change, doesn't enter into interaction with other shots, but the image arises by itself, from nowhere, as if it had preserved within itself hidden meanings.'

Muratova added two episodes to deepen Evgeniia's character and increase our sympathy for her by creating oblique, 'poetic' parallels. In the post office Evgeniia overhears Sasha's phone call to his father, confirming her worst fears. An elderly man asks her to take down the text of a letter: 'Dear Liusia and Gena! There in your far regions you are building your wonderful city. And we wait impatiently for you here, every day we get up and go to sleep with a single thought, to see you, our dear ones, as soon as possible.' As Evgeniia patiently takes his dictation, we and she realise the potential parallels between his situation and her lonely future. Later in the film she reminisces about an incident when she and Sasha's father came across a red parrot in a tree. 'Someone forgot to close the door of his cage. So he flew out. And he didn't plan to go anywhere. I'm curious, does your father remember that or not? [...] Ask him and write to me.' The parrot is a thinly disguised stand-in for Sasha, fleeing from his cage (their shared room) without really knowing where he's going. In her request to write, she is acknowledging, and accepting, his decision to go.

In the brilliant final episode, at an office party, their roles are reversed. Evgeniia is reduced to childish hysteria by the prospect of Sasha's 'desertion' as she shows him off to her colleagues. When they find others sitting in their assigned seats she returns again and again, like the raccoon in Flaherty's film, to reclaim them, creating an embarrassing scene. Izvolova points out that 'In the film's finale, the heroine, with the help of a simple human gesture, repeats Muratova's cinematic gesture. It is not the director who repeats shots of the film, but the heroine who can't stop herself and keeps returning to one and the same repeated action.'[32] Sasha leads her out to the garden, where, in tears, she takes off the brunette wig that makes her look too young for her years. The power of the final scene comes from the sudden removal of their masks, signalled by Evgeniia's removal of her wig and Sasha's plain and sincere language: 'I love you, Mama, I won't leave.' The camera is merciless in its harsh close-ups of Sharko's ageing yet still attractive face, with her smudged mascara. Earlier in the film it had been equally ruthless in watching her make herself up, putting on the false face she shows to the world, behind which she has lost sight of her own identity. In the background a young girl sings an amateur rendition of Lermontov's endlessly anthologised poem 'The Sail' ('And he, restless one, seeks the storm, as if in the storm he will find peace') – an ironic commentary on Evgeniia's view of her son, while the on-camera action demonstrates how mistaken she is. Shilova and Plakhov both attribute broader social meaning to the ending, though they read it differently. In

Evgeniia's defence of her seat, Shilova sees 'a despairing duel of the heroine with "man" in general, for the right to occupy the "place" of which she has been deprived for ever'.[33] For Plakhov, the scene is remarkable because the son suddenly sees in his mother 'a lonely human being, who, more than anything else in life, needs affection. Sharko's heroine is also the Soviet people, which, in their condition of inborn neurosis, really ask so little to be happy.'[34]

In April 1995 Muratova returned to the United States for a festival of glasnost-era films at Lincoln Center's Walter Reade Theater. *New York Times* critic Janet Maslin was enthusiastic about *The Long Farewell*, which opened the series. 'Moody and hypnotic in its portrait of a smart, vibrant woman flailing desperately against her own disillusionment and the fraying of family ties, it suggests a subversively negative look at every turn. The director noted that Soviet censors complained that extras in the party scene were not smiling as happily as they should.'[35]

In 1976, five years after her 'disqualification', the Odessa Studio suggested Muratova try a screen version of a classic, since she 'didn't know how to film contemporary themes'. At first, she recalls, she didn't want to, 'but then I re-read Lermontov's *Hero of Our Time*. I hadn't read it in school, it wasn't shopworn in my consciousness.[36] I took [the section] "Princess Mary" and I was astounded by its illusoriness and sense of being "beyond the looking glass".' She cast Natalia Leble and Yuri Shlykov in the leading roles and began screen tests, but the administration didn't like them, they found 'contemporizing' and 'allusions' and shut down the production.[37] Zorky recalls that in the mid-1970s, in Odessa, he was shown those screen tests for *Princess Mary* 'From underground, as a rare treasure...They reminded me of an album of swift, impetuous, and acute sketches and revealed such an original approach to the theme that it couldn't help but sow fear in the hearts of her "minders".'[38]

# 3. The Unknown Muratova

In the eighteen years that separated *The Long Farewell* from *Asthenic Syndrome*, Muratova was able to complete only three films. These were her first films in colour, and they signal a marked shift in her visual style – from the verisimilitude of the two black and white 'melodramas' to a new phase that she herself describes as 'ornamentalism' (*dekorativnost'*). She worked with three different cinematographers, temporarily parting ways with Kariuk. *Getting to Know the Big, Wide World* was shot with Yuri Klimenko, who later worked with Paradjanov on *The Legend of Suram Fortress* [Legenda o Suramskoi kreposti, 1984]. Muratova has said that her acquaintance with the designer and director Rustam Khamdamov, who was to have been the costume designer on the aborted *Princess Mary*, marked a watershed in the look of her work.

> When he told me that a necklace shouldn't be filled with beads, but that here and there the thread should show through, that was a revelation for me, like Newton's apple... And I thought, 'That's how simple it is to show the construction of the world – that beads, it turns out, are threaded on a string.' That's when I began to be interested in the external side – costumes, ornamentalism.[1]

Liuba wears just such a necklace in *Getting to Know the Big, Wide World*. Muratova's second husband, artist and designer Evgeny Golubenko, who collaborated on all her films beginning with *A Change of Fate*, also contributed to the change in their visual style.

All three films encountered difficulties with distribution. *Getting to Know the Big, Wide World*, made at Lenfilm, was given extremely limited distribution after it displeased the studio bureaucrats; according to Muratova, only six prints were struck.[2] The authorities demanded such severe cuts in *Among the Grey Stones* that Muratova took her name off the picture. All restrictions were lifted for *A Change of Fate*, but the film was not released outside the USSR because the studio neglected to purchase the rights to the story from Maugham's heirs. I have been unable to find any contemporary Soviet reviews of either *Getting to Know the Big, Wide World* or *Among the Grey Stones*, and relatively few of *A Change of Fate*.

## *Getting to Know the Big, Wide World* [1978]

*Getting to Know the Big, Wide World* is a multicoloured, fancy-dress, almost phantasmagoric picture. When you watch it, it seems to have been made by another director.

Irina Shilova[3]

*Getting to Know the Big, Wide World* has received far less attention than its two predecessors. Undeservedly. Muratova has more than once called it her favourite film, and other critics, including this one, are partial to its charm and impish humour, as well as Muratova's cinematographic originality. Writing in a retrospective 1994 review, Zara Abdullaeva says: 'Without waiting for the rehabilitation of *Brief Encounters* and *The Long Farewell*, Muratova prepared for a fatal leap. She broke with the "provincial melodramas"... and made an outstanding film, in my opinion, her best.'[4] Muratova's bold leap combined two seemingly incompatible elements: the genuinely romantic story of Liuba's dawning love for the gentle Misha and the gaudy, theatricalised 'sots-art' world that surrounds them, of which Nikolai, Misha's rival, is the aggressive court jester. Plakhov calls the film 'the first specimen of socialist postmodernism'.[5] It was particularly courageous of Muratova, since the opportunity to shoot at Lenfilm, where her admirer Alexei German worked and had considerable influence, was an unexpected gift from above. Offered the choice of several scripts, Muratova chose an innocuous scenario by Grigori Baklanov about a romantic triangle at a construction site. The situation recalled Gerasimov's *Komsomolsk*: young volunteers building from scratch a new factory town, where they will settle and raise families. But Muratova's agenda was entirely different from that of the traditional construction film. She was fascinated by the aesthetic of the building site.

A building site is chaos – a sphere where culture has not yet been created, where there's no concept of 'beautiful/not beautiful,' where there's no aesthetic (it remains to be created). Chaos may seem terrible, but to me it is wonderful, because there are as yet no postulates at all. There's no style, so stylisation is impossible. I wanted to create a culture, a beauty outside existing canons.[6]

The film's intense colour palette begins with Liuba's garish red lipstick and continues with a huge bouquet of red roses at the end of the wedding ceremony, the red headscarves of the woman plasterers and the propaganda posters at the factory ceremony. This against a landscape of muddy, rutted roads and cramped, temporary housing.

The Lenfilm Studio Party Committee found her preliminary footage problematic because 'The excessively metaphoric quality of filmic language and an absorption with formal experiments eclipsed the content of an essentially simple story about awakening true love in the heroine's heart – love that elevates and ennobles her'.[7] GSRK urged the film-makers to continue work, 'proceeding from an aspiration towards simplicity, accessibility and genuine poetic quality'. At a meeting of the studio's Party Committee, Frida Gukasian, chief script editor of Lenfilm's first creative team, spoke in Muratova's defence.

> We are dealing with footage that is talented and out of the ordinary, so we must approach it all the more demandingly. [...] Kira Muratova was making a poem in prose, and that is one of the most difficult genres in our films. Its style is formed by a conjunction of the humdrum and the poetic, and sometimes these points of conjunction are missing.

Iosif Kheifets, artistic leader of Lenfilm's first creative team and director of a poetic version of Chekhov's *Lady With a Dog* [Dama s sobachkoi, 1960] expressed cautious optimism.

> This will be a film about spirituality of feeling, and about lack of spirituality – an extremely important theme. [...] Poeticization in our outlook on reality is unfamiliar to us, unfortunately... That passion, emotionality, and directorial

5.  *Getting to Know the Big, Wide World*: Nina Ruslanova, Sergei Popov

inventiveness which Kira Muratova is wasting on ornamentation needs to be aimed instead on the main subject – the relations between the characters.

Muratova answered the criticisms in a letter to F. Ermash, chairman of Goskino. 'My position... consists in the desire to make a film about love that is tender, selfless, and, most important, harmonious.'[8] Gukasian tried to put a conventional humanistic face on the finished film. 'The love story told in this film is not rich in plot events, but notable for its unusual characters, the complex web of relationships of three not-very-young people, the poetic intensity of the author's intonation.'[9]

*Getting to Know the Big, Wide World* featured three of Muratova's favourite actors: Nina Ruslanova (Liuba), Sergei Popov (Misha) and Natalia Leble (Galia), who was to have starred in the aborted *Princess Mary*. This was Popov's first appearance in a Muratova film; he would eventually appear in five altogether. Alexei Zharkov – like Ruslanova, at the beginning of a major acting career – played Nikolai. There was even a cameo appearance by super-star Liudmila Gurchenko, a classmate of Muratova's at VGIK.

Baklanov's scenario, incongruously titled 'The Birch Trees Whisper in the Breeze',[10] largely conformed to the canons of late Socialist Realism – little regret is voiced at the destruction of the village, which is 'living out its last days' at the edge of the construction site. The mud and disorder are treated as if the march of progress were unquestioned. Muratova used the scenario primarily as a springboard for improvisation, diverging further and further from it as the film progresses. Not surprisingly, Baklanov was not happy with what she did. 'He repudiated much of it, refused to accept it... But he agreed to co-authorship, and certain things he had to accept, perhaps not in their entirety, but there was nothing he could do.'[11] The character of Baklanov's heroine, the plasterer Liuba Nesmachnova, remains less defined than that of the two truck drivers who contend for her affection, Nikolai and the gentle newcomer Misha. She eventually realises that Misha wears a prosthesis below the knee, the result of a driving accident, but chooses him nevertheless. In Muratova's film Liuba occupies centre stage. If she is still a bit undefined, it is because she, like the life of the new factory city, is in the process of formation. While Baklanov's Liuba was a stock romantic object of desire, blonde and pretty with a sweet, unexceptional personality, Muratova's Liuba has a temper and a mind of her own. Baklanov's Nikolai was a familiar, relatively harmless, Russian male type: boastful, seeking to be the centre of attention, especially when under the influence. But Muratova darkens his image, adding incidents in which he demeans Liuba, verbally abuses her and pushes her around physically. Baklanov's Misha proved his worthiness not to Liuba but to society, in a display of selfless courage in which he saved a truckload of workers, a new mother and her baby. Muratova cuts that incident entirely. Her Misha is an eccentric, with his long, unruly curls, his milk drinking (Nikolai prefers a more traditional, transparent Russian beverage), his gentle manner and his respect for the village potter, an individual craftsman in a time of large-scale industry.

In Baklanov's version of the Komsomol wedding toast that Liuba gives on behalf of the social collective, 'someone with experience' gave her instructions. 'First you wish them happiness, as they say, and success in their work, and, so to speak, happiness in their personal life. Let them know that they are being congratulated not by just anyone, but by an outstanding worker.' She was constantly interrupted by the loudmouth Nikolai, and managed only to utter a few banalities. Muratova entirely transforms this crucial episode. She photographs Liuba from an extreme low angle as she stands radiant on the back of a truck, microphone in hand, trying to be heard over the din with her much-practised speech, a kind of working-class folk poetry.

> This is a great happiness! We are building such a big city, such a big factory! Houses can be big or they can be little, but that's not the most important thing, but more than anything else on earth it's important that the happiness be real! They don't manufacture it in factories, even on the best production lines. And if you've had the good fortune to fall in love, then you don't need anything else.

It is as if the laconic Nadia of *Brief Encounters*, played by a younger Ruslanova, has finally found her own voice. Swept along by her speech, Liuba turns coquettishly to Nikolai and asks, 'Do you love me?' He replies, cynically, 'Love is a temporary attraction, you know.' 'I know, Kolia, but I don't want to know,' she mumbles. Disheartened, she walks around to the back of the truck, repeating to herself: 'No one loves anyone [*Nikto nikogo ne liubit*].' This phrase became a crucial leitmotif in Muratova's films, a proposition she questioned in all of them; twenty-five years later, Ruslanova would speak the same words again, in a very different key, playing the bride's aunt in *Chekhov's Motifs*. Liuba pensively removes the blonde wig she has been wearing, and catches Misha's glance. She responds with a knowing, bitter-sweet expression, wiping away a tear. The newly-weds may not have been listening to her speech, but he was. Later in the film he speaks Liuba's words back to her, word for word, in the cab of his truck, using them shyly to declare his love.

Muratova films the Komsomol wedding as a kind of romantic grotesque. A loudspeaker announces, in the worst of Soviet rhetorical kitsch, 'Comrade brides, comrade grooms! Wrap it up! The Komsomol wedding is finished!' Multiple pairs of newly-weds, dressed in modest Soviet finery, kiss each other shyly, passionately and at length, in one of the few un-ironically romantic scenes in Muratova's cinema. In this film, at least, she is still trying to deny Liuba's pessimism about the possibility of love. She creates a delightful poetic episode in the village, where Misha parks his truck and teaches Liuba to play the harmonica. A baby in one of the windows evokes a dream sequence, in which Liuba sees herself, in bridal veil, riding a horse that Misha leads through the village. In another such addition Leble, playing Liuba's brigade chief Galya, dresses in a costume belonging to the local theatre troupe and declaims a monologue from Lermontov's 'Princess Mary', which she had prepared for her role in the aborted film; this was not the only time the 'housewifely' Muratova inserted suppressed material into a later film.

Baklanov wrote a sequence in which the headlights of Misha's passing truck fall on Liuba as Nikolai is forcing his attentions on her outside her trailer dormitory. Muratova takes the basic idea – the headlights of Misha's truck as the extension of his gaze – and makes of it something uniquely her own. Liuba (alone) is caught in the glare of the lights, which begin to flirt with her, turning on and off. She intuits that it is Misha, and records her pleasure with a little giggle. As the light remains glaringly on her she first tries shyly to defend herself, then, in a sequence repeated in five different versions, walks towards the source of the light, taking on this intimate interrogation, engaging with it, growing ever more serious. Muratova doubles a character for the first time, replacing Baklanov's young, naïve co-worker, aptly named Vera (Faith), with a pair of non-professional twins (Lena and Natasha Shelgunova). In a hilarious scene, one twin reads the ritual speech at the dedication of a factory building, while the other prompts her when she forgets her lines.

Muratova mischievously put a paragraph of grandiloquent prose from Baklanov's narrator into Nikolai's mouth. After the three visit the potter's workshop he stands on the bumper of Misha's truck and loudly declaims: 'For contemporary man a plane flying in the sky and a rocket in smoke and flames, tearing itself away from the earth on the screens of thousands of television sets – all this is a familiar sight. But how many people in our day have seen a potter at work?' To make sure we catch her satiric view of this performance, Muratova places a chicken in the foreground (a rooster would be an even better commentary, but Muratova never overdoes her sight gags). At the end of the film, when Misha asks Liuba to come with him to ZAGS (the marriage registration office) to secure their place in 'the longest line in town', he brings her, as an engagement present, a small, hand-thrown vase.

Zlobina and Karasev have noted in the early films of both Muratova and German the seemingly paradoxical relationship between their psychological and physical true-to-life quality and the theatricalisation of their characters' speech. 'The people on the screen seem to do the same things as in life, but with the difference that the most expressive elements of life – jokes, singing, practical jokes, tears, laughter – become the core of the heroes' behaviour. [...] Theatricalization turns out to be the peculiar "price" for the cinema's striving for trueness to life.'[12]

Absolutely authentic everyday speech comes across as dull and undramatic on the screen. So, they argue, to retain the quality of authenticity Muratova and German choose to film the naturally expressive moments of everyday speech. Both Muratova's previous films began with just such theatricalised speech. Valentina segues from her unfinished speech on agriculture into her parodies of Shakespeare and Mozart and the two-part conversation she performs all by herself. *The Long Farewell* begins with a mini-lecture by two shop girls explaining the hydroponic culture of plants. Evgeniia's entire character is built on the theatricality of her speech: her oft-told story about her father, her flirtatious conversation with Nikolai Sergeevich at the dacha, her confrontation with her boss, her long monologue about the red parrot – all seem to be spoken as if an audience is listening. The dialogue in *Getting to Know the Big, Wide World* is equally theatricalised. In the opening shots Nikolai hails Misha's truck to help pull his Zhiguli out of the mud, but can't resist launching into a satiric imitation of an advertisement for the tiny car: 'Speed, comfort, ability to handle a variety of roads, manoeuvrability...' Liuba is first heard off-screen, rehearsing the speech she is to make at the wedding. Misha, seeing her for the first time, launches into an uncharacteristically long monologue about how she reminds him of a woman who ran out suddenly onto the road as he was driving with his instructor. Shilova analyses the link between language and the Soviet social context in the film.

> People... have been taught to tread the indicated road, utter memorized speeches, take part in public events [*meropriiatiakh*] that, to say it plainly, take up the greater part of their lives. And that life itself has turned into a peculiar theatre. The individual has been erased. Everything is subject to the stage direction of mass celebrations, holidays, Komsomol weddings. Spectacle has swallowed up life.[13]

## *Among the Grey Stones* [1983]

> *Among the Grey Stones* leads us into a world of lost integrity, into a world in which humanity is totally lost, a world without women.
>
> Irina Shilova[14]

For Soviet film-makers, screen versions of literary classics, both Russian and foreign, often provided a safe haven in times of particularly troublesome censorship. Given the criticisms heaped on her first three films for their 'incorrect' treatment of contemporary life, it is not surprising that she adapted her next two from literary works. *Among the Grey Stones* is set in nineteenth-century Russia, *A Change of Fate* among British colonials in Singapore. Muratova based *Among the Grey Stones* on Vladimir Korolenko's classic 1885 story for children, 'In Bad Company'. Korolenko, a populist who ran foul of the tsarist censorship, wrote it in the early 1880s in Siberian exile and finished it in St Petersburg during a short stay in jail. A sentimental tear-jerker that asserts the moral worth of society's poor and rejected, it was required reading for sixth-graders in the Soviet school curriculum.[15] The story is narrated in the first person by the central character, Vasia, now an adult. When he was six, his mother died of tuberculosis. His father, a judge, was so overcome with grief that he was unable to express his love for his son. Vasia took to sneaking out of the house, wandering the town with friends. He discovered a brother and sister, Valek and Marusia, who lived with their father, Pan Tiburtsius, and a gang of beggars and tramps in the underground vaults of an abandoned chapel. These are the 'grey stones' of the film's title, which are 'sucking the life' out of little Marusia. Vasia befriends them, bringing apples from his garden and other treats.

Vasia's comfortable world-view is shaken when he realises that the children and their friends in the underground have to steal to survive. He is particularly fond of Marusia. When the rainy autumn comes, her illness takes a turn for the worse. Vasia asks his younger sister to lend him her large porcelain doll, a gift from their late mother. To their surprise, Marusia lights up at the sight of the doll and even seems to improve. But its disappearance causes a scandal at home, and Vasia, despite intense pressure, refuses to tell his father where it is. In the midst of this interrogation, Tiburtsius comes to return the doll; Marusia has died. Taking the judge aside, he tells him of Vasia's compassionate deeds. The judge asks his son's forgiveness and vows to give him the attention and love he so craves. He allows him to say farewell to Marusia, sending money and a friendly warning for the family to leave town, for Tiburtsius is wanted on some (unspecified) matter for which punishment would have to be exacted if he appeared in court. The tale's villain is Janusz (who prefers the Frenchified 'Jean'), the former butler of the local Polish aristocracy, who drove Tiburtsius and his friends out of the ruins of the lordly castle, and tries to denounce them (and Vasia) to the judge.

Muratova adapted the story into a screenplay in the 1970s simply for the money, not intending to film it herself. But in the early 1980s it seemed to provide a safe vehicle for her first film at the Odessa Studio since the scandal over *The Long Farewell* and the closing of *Princess Mary*. Even this canonised story, however, turned out to be politically problematic, given the nascent national movements in the Soviet Union. Korolenko set his tale in a small town in what is now western Ukraine. A half-ruined Uniate (Ukrainian Catholic) chapel, surrounded by a graveyard, and the ruins of the castle of the former Polish lordly family testify to the town's history as part of the Kingdom of Poland. The large Jewish population of tradespeople locates it within the pale of settlement as well. The town's multi-ethnic and multi-religious composition,

which Korolenko explained in detail, is papered over in the film. The Jews
are nowhere to be seen. The Uniate chapel becomes in the dialogue lists
simply a 'castle', though the huge crucifix on the wall makes its real nature
clear. Korolenko's obviously Polish 'Pan Tiburtsius Drab' has become in the
film the thoroughly Russian 'Valentin'. In the original story, the mysteriously
well-educated Pan Tiburtsius constantly spouted Latin phrases and declaimed
long passages from Latin authors. It was rumoured that he absorbed the
Jesuits' lessons better than the young master whose boots he was sent to polish.
In the film it is clear that Valentin is well-educated, but Latin – indicating a
Catholic (i.e. Polish) education – does not pepper his speech.[16]

Muratova kept very little of Korolenko's wordy dialogue, though the film
follows the outlines of the story reasonably faithfully. But she radically
subverted the sentimental style of the original to produce an alienated,
distanced, even somewhat ironic version of the children's classic. This is the
first film in which, rather than simply choosing theatricalised moments of
everyday speech, she significantly deformed characters' speech through
repetition. Hardly anyone in the film speaks naturally: the denizens of the
underground engage in lunatic or drunken rants, the judge (played by Stanislav
Govoriukhin, the Odessa Studio's most successful director) strides through

6. *Among the Grey Stones*: Stanislav Govoriukhin

the house ordering the removal of anything that reminds him of his wife, and the nurse, played by an almost unrecognisable Ruslanova, is in a constant pitch of hysteria. Vasia (Igor Sharapov) speaks in a high, reedy and sometimes expressionless voice, which at first alienates us from the boy rather than evoking sympathy. Marusia (Oksana Shlapak) is played by an adult dwarf, making her seem unnaturally mature for her years. The repetition of words and phrases is most intense in Marusia's speech, which is mechanical rather than childlike.

It is hard to know how much of Muratova's original vision was destroyed by the unauthorised cuts made before its release. She recalls that the sections cut were each rather large, and centred in the depiction of the 'underground'.[17] 'They wanted the poor to be poor only to a certain degree, that pre-revolutionary Russia be painted in softer colours... The situation was truly absurd. I asked them, "Why was it necessary to have the revolution and shed all that blood if old Russia was, in the end, acceptable?"'[18] Instead of Korolenko's leisurely introductory biographies of the underground's lunatics and alcoholics, *Among the Grey Stones* begins directly with the father/son relationship. Vasia, climbing a huge, magnificently photographed tree in the garden, tries to get the attention of his sobbing father below. Preoccupied with his grief, the judge seems to be reading from a script of fatherly conduct. 'Do you remember your mother?' he asks, in a voice devoid of emotion. 'Have you done your homework, Sir?' he continues, switching ironically into highly formal and archaic language totally inappropriate for a father addressing his young son. Later in the film Vasia gains the courage to reply that it is summer and he has no lessons. Human communication grows increasingly difficult in Muratova's films; exchanges between her characters are more and more often performances rather than conversation. As he climbs further, Vasia replays his father's questions in his head. The answer comes by way of the mother's off-screen voice: 'Things don't obey me. How heavy the spoon is! It's impossible to open the window, to take a child on my knee. Here's a yellow flower, here's a red flower, here's a white flower. What a heavy blue flower! The flower is heavier than the spoon! And here's blood. I'm afraid of blood. I'll give you binoculars, and I'll give Sonechka a wonderful doll, so you children will remember their mama.' The monologue is Muratova's, not Korolenko's, and the voice that reads it is hers as well. The flowers, which we have already seen piled around the mother's grave, play an ominous, though somewhat different, role in story and film. In Korolenko's story flowers are the favourite plaything of Marusia, whom he describes as herself like a flower that had grown in the absence of sunlight. In *Among the Grey Stones* shots of wilting roses in vases behind a creaking door appear three times with no evident diegetic meaning other than to signal the mother's recent death and the grief in the house. Shilova notes that this is the first Muratova film with no central adult female character. Its drama centres, instead, around her absence, as father and son try to reconstitute their relationship without the mother.

As Vasia nears the top of the tree he uses binoculars, his mother's last gift, to observe the 'humiliated and insulted'. They are being expelled by Jean and his ally, the police chief, from the ruined castle. The style of the scene is grotesque chaos: the police chief's order is estranged by a denizen of the castle, who loudly repeats each phrase after him. Behind a veil of smoke, a close-cropped pair of coughing lunatics sings stanzas from Pushkin's endlessly anthologised poem 'Winter Evening'. When the alcoholic self-styled 'General' Turkevich repeatedly proclaims 'I forbid everything', it is tempting to see Muratova grinning from behind the mask of Korolenko's high-minded sentiments, thumbing her nose at her persecutors in the cultural bureaucracy.

In the midst of the chaos, Valentin (Popov) makes his first entrance. He is a non-stop talker, or – more accurately – performer, for his literary monologues are usually addressed to no one in particular. The unctuous Jean offers to make an exception and let him stay, but Valentin disdainfully refuses. The episode evokes Vasia's first expression of social consciousness. Valentin will later teach Vasia something else of great importance: the father from whom he is alienated is actually one of the town's few admirable men, having refused a bribe from a rich nobleman. In a sequence of Muratova's invention, Valentin, shadowed by Vasia and a pack of curious boys, leads his motley troupe of refugees to shelter in the abandoned chapel. There is something Christ-like about his demeanour, reinforced by an elaborately choreographed procession among the crosses of the graveyard. 'Conformity is the law of life,' he declares ironically – another Muratova line that lends itself to Aesopian interpretation. She juxtaposes this scene of madmen to the hysteria in the judge's house.

The film is a visual feast, the *mise en scène* rich with the grey stones of the ruined castle and the Catholic chapel. The rags of the homeless are examined with the same interest as the mud and disorder of the building site in *Getting to Know the Big, Wide World*. When Vasia steals into his sister's room to take the doll (he does not, as in the story, ask her permission) he has to pick her out of a pile of thirty or so dolls, all smiling with a grotesque rigidity. Symbolically laden dolls appear in nearly every one of Muratova's films, and Elena Stishova calls them the 'trademark, the brand' of her poetics.[19] There is a brief shot of a doll in Evgeniia Vasilevna's room in *The Long Goodbye*; they later appear in *Asthenic Syndrome*, *The Sentimental Policeman*, *Three Stories* and *Letter to America*. The doll and flower motifs combine in the opening shot of *Asthenic Syndrome* – dried flowers and a broken doll on a rubbish heap. What does Muratova mean by these recurring dolls? In *Among the Grey Stones* the beautiful porcelain doll was an important element of the original story's plot. But, by surrounding her with so many others, Muratova does more than simply contrast the wealth of the judge's house with the poverty of the underground. She is defamiliarising the very notion of 'doll', asking us to look afresh at this symbol of childhood love and innocence as a rigidly lifeless substitute for a human being. Except for the elegantly dressed doll in this film, which is briefly held in Marusia's embrace, the dolls in Muratova's other films are plastic, naked, alone and unloved. They seem a visual equivalent of Muratova's repeated question: does anyone love anyone?

The studio insisted on substantial cuts. 'The reasons were so stupid that I feel ill talking about them,' Muratova recalls.[20] Even the title was changed, from Muratova's 'Children of the Underground' to the more ambiguous 'Among the Grey Stones', the title of one section of the original story. 'When I found out, I raced off to Moscow and Kiev. I announced that if they made those cuts I would take my name off the titles […] I thought that this would stop them, but it didn't. Several scenes were cut out and destroyed.'[21] The film was released with Ivan Sidorov (the Russian equivalent of Joe Bloggs) listed as the director. Ironically, this least-known, and most butchered, of Muratova's films was the only one to be shown at Cannes. In May 1988 it appeared in the non-competition rubric 'Un certain regard'. The film evidently disappointed the expectations of her new French fans, who wanted another women's film like *Brief Encounters* and *The Long Goodbye*. Puzzled critics who caught *Among the Grey Stones* at Cannes wrote a few brief reviews. 'It remains, despite the massacre, a touching work, imperfect, vaguely bizarre, almost irreal.'[22] A review ecstatically titled 'Kira Muratova Slavissimo' declared the film 'beautiful like a Slavonic liturgy, baroque like a Gesualdo motet'.[23] The reviewer for *Positif* complained that the director had not plunged deeply into the psychology of either adults or children, leaving the audience 'rather cold to the ethical conflict that should have sustained this contemplative story'.[24] Its screening at Cannes resulted from another of those grotesque ironies in Muratova's professional life. Originally, the studio planned to send her newest film, *A Change of Fate*. But the Odessa Studio had 'omitted' to buy the rights to the story from Maugham's heirs.[25] 'They didn't simply forget, it just never entered their minds that they needed to buy the rights,' Muratova explains.[26]

## *A Change of Fate* [1987]

> A Change of Fate…is Muratova's most decadent film (outrageously gloomy and stylistically old-fashioned). At the time, it appeared the caprice of an artist who didn't know what to do with her newly-granted freedom.
>
> Andrei Plakhov[27]

In Maugham's original story, 'The Letter' (1927), Leslie Crosbie, the seemingly proper wife of a British planter in Singapore, murders her lover, Geoff Hammond, in a fit of jealousy and tries to claim it was an act of self-defence against rape. Her account is undermined by the appearance of a frenzied note she had written him that day, begging him to come to see her in her husband's absence. The note is in the possession of Hammond's Chinese concubine. When Mr Joyce, her lawyer, confronts her with its contents, Leslie changes her story, claiming she had in fact invited Hammond to drop by to give her advice on a rifle she wanted to buy for her husband as a surprise birthday present. Joyce advises her that the passionate tone of the letter contradicts such a version, and would increase suspicion about the only weak link in her defence: the fact that she had shot Hammond not once but six times, emptying the revolver over him in evident fury. Leslie's blindly devoted husband Robert agrees to ransom the letter for a sum representing nearly all his assets; the court acquits Leslie. The kernel of Maugham's story is in Joyce's observation that 'You can never tell what hidden possibilities of savagery there are in the most respectable of women'.

The paradoxical character of a seemingly meek and upstanding British colonial wife who turns out to be a femme fatale inspired several adaptations of the story, including Maugham's own stage version and a popular 1940 American film, *The Letter*, directed by William Wyler and starring Bette Davis. Muratova claims that she knew neither of these, and was simply basing herself on Maugham's story, which she had proposed several times before: 'I was fond of the situation with the note ... I wanted a kind of eclecticism – some unde-fined Eastern country, a colony, a colonial, without any particular national identity – just natives and colonials, as a sign.'[28] The enigma of the heroine's character remains at the centre of Muratova's film. But rather than simply replicate the realistic style of Maugham's story, Muratova took it as a pre-text, which she translated into a radically different key, far closer to surrealism, adding elements of the grotesque.

Muratova shifted the locale from Singapore (where, in any case, the Odessa Studio could not afford to send her on location) to an unspecified locale in Central Asia.[29] Her main characters speak Russian, though, except for the husband, their physical appearance and dress are generically European rather than Russian or Soviet. The husband, with his little goatee and fur-trimmed coat, seems to have stepped out of a Dostoevsky novel. The names Muratova gave them are international: Leslie Crosbie (played by Leble, whose face has the uncanny ability to move from prim innocence to demonic passion in the flicker of an eye) becomes Maria, Maria's lover (Leonid Kudriashov) is Alexander, and her husband (Vladimir Karasev) Filip/Philip. Mr Joyce (Shlykov) is identified only as 'the lawyer'. Leble and Shlykov were to have played the leads in *Princess Mary*, and Plakhov sees this film's 'attempt to penetrate into the secret hiding places of human consciousness and subconscious' as 'a lament of the author for the beautiful child not born in its own time'. Leble, he explains, was discovered for the cinema by Khamdamov, who so influenced Muratova's visual style.[30] During the 1970s and 1980s Leble was married to an American journalist, and she lived with him in the Philippines during his posting there. Her return to Russia to act in *A Change of Fate* was a sign of the changing possibilities under Gorbachev.

Maugham's story is narrated in the third person from Joyce's point of view. His reader doesn't encounter the enigmatic Mrs Crosbie in person until nearly halfway through the story, when Joyce visits her in jail to ask about the rumoured note. Muratova gave much more screen time and dialogue to Maria. While Maugham filtered Leslie's original account of the murder through Joyce's retelling, Muratova let Maria narrate her own fiction. She kept most of Maugham's dialogue, but estranged it by having the actors recite it at a faster than normal pace, often with minimal expression. She added several

7. *A Change of Fate*: Natalia Leble, Leonid Kudriashov (photo credit: A. Roizman)

totally new episodes, which are the moments in the film where she gives full rein to the grotesque. Until Leslie is confronted with the letter, Maugham's reader is led to see her through the eyes of Mr Joyce as 'the last woman in the world to commit murder' – a crucial sentence that, in retrospect, the reader notices that Maugham isolated in a paragraph of its own. Her fiction about consulting Hammond about the rifle[31] was introduced only halfway through Maugham's original story.

Muratova, on the other hand, chose to begin her film with this lie and Maria's rehearsal of it. The visual images that open *A Change of Fate* represent Maria's initial version of the event, while the soundtrack presents her second account, following the discovery of the letter. Maria, in a bright red sweater and sequined black harlequin mask, reclines in a chair. 'And so, awakened by an audacious kiss…' begins an off-screen female voice, its flat, emotionless tone in sharp contrast to the event she describes. We hear an off-screen, non-diegetic wolf howl. A male voice enters the dialogue.

> He: You [intimate second person singular] wanted to get my advice about a
>     present.
> She: Now I don't want to.
> He: You wanted to give your husband a rifle.

This is the verbal theme the variations and recapitulations of which will form the fugue-like score of the opening sequence. In a long tracking shot, a handsome man in a light-coloured suit guides Maria by the hand down a steep, circular staircase inside a conservatory filled with lush tropical foliage. He presses his attentions on her, and we hear sounds of struggle. But the emotionless dialogue continues on the voice-over: the woman uses the formal second person plural in addressing the man; he replies in the second person singular, implying an intimate relationship. The rapidly moving shots keep the viewer disoriented, as does the exotic location. Who are these people? Where are they? What is their relationship? It is not immediately clear whether the voice-over is an accurately recalled flashback or a product of Maria's imagination. Muratova puts her viewer in the same quandary as Maria's lawyer; the film's narrative thread is as tangled as the yarn in the lace Maria is always working on.

The second episode leaves the viewer just as disoriented. Maria is in a large, vaulted prison cell, washing up with the help of an elderly, mute native servant. This sequence is cinematically as bare as the first was ornamental. It is the bizarre speech of the warder and the actions of Maria's fellow prisoners that now draw our attention. The warder, with a mane of silvery hair and an eye for the ladies, enters Maria's cell and calmly recites a long racist screed as if there were nothing at all objectionable in it. 'We are all civilized people, *white* people; we should be friends, united in solidarity. I can't endure native women – only a white woman is a woman. That is, they are – strictly speaking – also white, but sort of yellowish. You are a real treat for us. It's been a long time since there was a white woman in this prison.'[32] Maria paces back and forth while the camera remains static; though imprisoned, she now seems to be the active force, rather than the passive object of desire in the opening sequences. She works on her lace, with an expression of polite agreement, or at least acquiescence, to her warder's peroration. Her hair is done up in a school-marmish bun, and she wears large-framed glasses (much like those in which Muratova was often photographed at the same period), in stark contrast to her more provocative appearance in the opening scene. The warder's assistant escorts into the cell an unlikely trio of inmates, who perform circus acts for her – 'a little concert, a divertissement, an amusement for ladies'. The performers, according to Muratova,[33] were originally cut from *Among the Grey Stones*. She was so fond of them that she re-shot the episode and placed it here with little or no diegetic motivation. It is a perfect example of homage to the exaggerated acting style of FEKS, the manifesto of which urged the adaptation of the circus aesthetic to film.

Finally, Muratova takes up Maugham's narrative. The lawyer's consultation with Maria's husband, for the most part, follows Maugham, but its beginning is more emotional and Dostoevskian in pitch. 'It's a mockery!' exclaims Filip. Maugham's Mr Crosbie offered instead the decidedly British: 'You know, it is a damned shame that they should have arrested her.' Halfway through the conversation, an exotic violin melody intrudes on the soundtrack, just as the lawyer is saying: 'But the fact remains that murder has been committed, and in a civilized community a trial is inevitable.' His outer office is a scene of 'oriental' confusion; two men talking simultaneously at cross-purposes, two in native costume squatting on the floor with a sheep, and the lawyer's foppish clerk (Umirzak Shmanov) carefully examining a ring, perhaps his payment for acting as intermediary in the blackmail scheme. Except for the jail servant this is the viewer's first glimpse of the 'natives', and the scene contrasts the 'Asian chaos' with the lawyer's attempt to maintain the rationality of European law.

Muratova invented an episode in which Filip, three of Maria's well-dressed lady friends and her dwarf, deaf-mute ward (Shlapak) visit her in jail. The sequence is full of unexplained eccentric elements, perhaps best understood as Eisenstinian 'attractions': a comic debate between the two warders about who ordered coffee for the visitors; a guard patrolling the wall, making obscene gestures; and Maria's own entrance, dressed in furs and swaggering in the manner of Katerina Izmailova, the adulterous murderess from Shostakovich's opera and the Leskov story 'Lady Macbeth of Mtsensk'. Ignoring her husband, Maria turns with animation and affection to her ward. They have a lengthy conversation in sign language, during which Maria's face takes on expressions of sincere affection never seen elsewhere in the film. While Maugham's Crosbie is pitiable in his loyalty, Muratova's Filip is comically ridiculous. But Muratova claimed that, of all the characters, this tragi-comic husband was the most sympathetic for her.

During Maria's interview with the lawyer the camera is at first mobile, mirroring her behaviour, by turns distracted and flirtatious. But, as she begins to recount the murder, the camera freezes for extremely long static shots, in stark contrast to the visual retelling of the story at the beginning of the film. There is a flashback to the murder scene, with Alexander's body lying on the floor and the wail of a manservant heard in the background. At this point the visual environment of the film shifts markedly to Central Asia. We have seen very few of the natives, and heard them hardly at all. Now the white colonial lies dead, the ward is mute, and the natives are finally given a voice. The scene is followed by a long, beautiful sequence of Alexander's horse escaping past the mountains into the desert, the only sounds the noise of its hoofs and the howl of a wolf – an eerie echo of the opening sequence. When the clerk produces a copy of the letter and offers to help ransom it, agency has shifted from the colonials to the natives, and this atmosphere of 'oriental chaos', noted by Susan Larsen, continues to grow till the end of the film, first in a dance hall, where the lawyer convinces Filip to ransom the letter, then in a wild trip to the village where the native concubine lives.

An intertitle announces that the court has acquitted Maria, and her society friends gather to celebrate. One of the ladies exclaims: 'I love it when some-one loves someone!' – an ironic echo of Liuba's 'No one loves anyone' in *Getting to Know the Big, Wide World*. But (and here, again, Muratova departs from Maugham) Filip excuses himself and leaves early. Burning the fateful letter, Maria confesses the details of her affair to the lawyer. Muratova cuts to a shot of kittens playing with dangling shoelaces. They are those of Filip's corpse; he has hanged himself in the stable. The ward, glimpsed in the doorway, is for the second time a silent witness to the death of a man fated to be involved with this 'most respectable of women'. The film ends with long shots of Filip's horse running free into the desert as the soundtrack reprises a monologue from Maria's diary: 'Since a certain happy time, I have been visited by a spirit or a demon, or an incubus… I don't know how to call it, perhaps an angel.' Then it switches to a reprise of Filip's monologue about the bewitching beauty of the guns he collects.

Though *A Change of Fate* was Muratova's first film to benefit from the new freedoms of the Gorbachev era, it represents more a change of aesthetics than of politics. Visually it is a very busy film, with details that are often left for the viewer to decode, just as a prosecutor looks everywhere for clues. Its distinctive look undoubtedly owes something to Golubenko, credited with the somewhat unusual title of 'decorator'. The neo-primitivist paintings on the walls of both Maria's house and the house of the native concubine are in his distinctive style. The film intensifies other elements that would characterise the second half of Muratova's oeuvre: repetition, unnatural speech, black humour. In *A Change of Fate* rehearsed speech occupies centre stage, for the story is *about* lying, about the heroine's false version of the murder, which will eventually be 'played' in court. Each of Muratova's first three films explored a woman's character in terms of her relationships with others – Valentina with Maxim and Nadia, Evgeniia with her son Sasha, Liuba with Nikolai and Mikhail. By lying about the circumstances of Alexander's death, Maria cuts herself off from all intimate relationships, except that with her ward. From this film on, human relationships in Muratova's films become ever more attenuated; communication is reduced to a minimum as characters talk past, rather than to, each other.

Plakhov's review in the August 1988 issue of *Film Art* was the first of a Muratova film in that most important Russian cinema journal in twenty years. Though he praises her work, he clearly finds this film hard to understand or place in social context. He confesses that 'a well-worn idealism led us to hope that precisely Muratova, precisely now, would make a film that would be in the best sense "relevant", that would embody the change of her own artistic fate and – as a result – a new quality of artistic thinking, about which we can only dream'.[34] His title, 'A Change of Decoration', reveals his disappointment. 'Before us, it seems to me, is a film of crisis, transitional, internally dissonant.' On the other hand, he insists that 'those who say that this is programmatically decadent, portraying humanity after the fall and therefore hopelessly pessimistic, have understood nothing in it'. Writing three years later, Aleksandr Shpagin disagrees. 'This prophetic film foresaw today's reality. It caught the atmosphere of breakdown, disorder, which unfolded two years later.'[35] And Shilova pronounces it 'Perhaps Muratova's most prophetic film... A world trying to be resurrected receives a heavy legacy from the past.'[36]

The critical response revealed the predicament of a long-repressed director whose twenty-year-old films were being rediscovered by a public that wanted more of the same. Muratova had changed, and so had the times. As it soon became clear in *Asthenic Syndrome*, she was able to reflect brilliantly on those times in her art. But not yet. While there is much of interest in *A Change of Fate*, it does have flaws. There are many elements in the film that do not coalesce even after multiple viewings. Perhaps the sudden freedom offered Muratova was too heady, and she temporarily lost the focus that earlier restrictions had imposed on her.

# 4. Soviet Apocalypse: *Asthenic Syndrome* [1990]

In Muratova's film we clearly taste the approaching catastrophe, or rather the catastrophe that has already begun.

Boris Vladimirsky[1]

Writing in 1991, just before the fall of the USSR, Plakhov declared that *Asthenic Syndrome* is 'a film that, in fact, closes the cine-epoch of the 1980s. And perhaps, not only of the 1980s.'[2] What Plakhov sensed, but could not yet say, is that the film heralded both the end of Soviet cinema and of Soviet society. In *Asthenic Syndrome*, Muratova's triumph is in making apocalypse palpable. Although the weakness syndrome from which the main characters suffer is particularly symbolic of Soviet society in its death throes, Muratova's message is more general: 'I don't see any fundamental difference between us and the West. Mankind is everywhere, in general, the same. I see in the world a level of suffering and cruelty that surpasses understanding.' But these qualities, Muratova feels, are more visible in Soviet life because 'in a poor man, a hungry man, in an insecure man, this cruelty is more evident, his anger is on the surface, this structure, this skeleton, is laid bare'. She describes asthenia as 'a condition of nervous exhaustion, resulting in inappropriate behaviour or lack of affect'.[3] Elsewhere, she elaborates: 'In the olden days it was called hypochondria, or black melancholia. Each time Nikolai (Sergi Popov) cannot cope with circumstances, he falls asleep. In the end, he falls asleep for good.'[4] The syndrome afflicts the central characters in the film as well as the society in which they live. Natasha (Olga Antonova), grief-stricken, rejects the sympathy of her friends and co-workers, and fights with strangers on the street. 'Natasha masochistically wants to draw out her suffering, while taking revenge on others because they continue to live as if nothing were wrong, while she is in torment,' observes Liubov' Paikova. 'Nikolai has also suffered an irrevocable loss,' she continues; 'he has lost himself.'[5]

*Asthenic Syndrome* confronts and challenges the viewer, continually frustrating narrative expectations. Seemingly unstructured, it is built from a series of episodes involving and observed by her two main characters, which add up to a portrait of the era. The episodes form two stylistically distinct narratives, linked thematically by the psychological and physical syndrome from which both characters suffer and structurally by rhyming images and episodes.[6] The first story is a film within a film, lasting approximately forty minutes, centred on Natasha, a doctor who has just lost her husband and is emotionally paralysed by her grief. This section is shot in black and white, like Muratova's first two 'provincial melodramas', and Plakhov rightly calls it 'a bitter and ironic paraphrase of Muratova's previous self'.[7] Nikolai, the central character of the longer second section, filmed in colour, is an ineffectual high school English teacher who would rather be a writer, and escapes from an unbearable world by falling asleep in inappropriate places.

Natasha and Nikolai, counter to the traditions of the Russian intelligentsia, have abdicated their professional responsibilities. Natasha refuses to help her neighbour's sick wife and tries to resign from her post at the hospital. Nikolai walks away from his chaotic classroom. Muratova intentionally reverses sex role stereotypes: Natasha displays an unfeminine aggression, Nikolai an unmanly passivity. Each toys with a wildly inappropriate sexual relationship – Natasha with a drunk from the street, Nikolai with a precocious pupil. Both find it difficult to go on with a life devoid of meaning, although they react in opposite ways. In the morally and aesthetically distorted world that surrounds Nikolai, social bonds are so attenuated that father fights with daughter, wife with husband, and teacher with pupil.

Although many censorship restrictions had been relaxed by the time *Asthenic Syndrome* was completed in 1989, the authorities took particular exception to the sequence near the end of the film in which a well-dressed woman in a subway car emits a lengthy stream of vulgar language (what Russians call *mat*) directed straight at the viewer. Pressure was put on Muratova to cut this brief scene, or muffle the words with train noise so that the film could be released, but she adamantly refused. The film's release was delayed for nearly six months. Ironically, it became the last shelved film of the Soviet era, not for its devastating picture of Soviet society but because of these 'unprintable' words, which are Muratova's reaction to that devastation. Asked why this sequence was so important to her, she replies:

> First, this is simply the truth of life, straightforward realism. Vulgar language accompanies my life from the moment I step outside my house. As I walk along the streets, it accompanies me like birdsong or the rustle of leaves ... If I had

reflected the real scale of the phenomenon, it would have sounded uninterrupted during the length of the entire film.[8]

In their daily life, Russians, particularly working-class males, speak in a language that could never pass the puritan standards of the Soviet censor. It began to appear in print only quite late in the glasnost era, and *Asthenic Syndrome* was taboo-breaking in Soviet cinema.[9] Though some viewers were offended by the scene of dogs in a pound waiting to be put down, the nudity (including male frontal nudity) in the film was not even mentioned in the critical debate; other late Soviet film-makers had already rushed to take advantage of this particular freedom for less exalted purposes.

Three writers are credited with the screenplay: Popov, Alexander Chernykh and Muratova. The young screenwriter Chernykh contributed the twist that holds the two parts together: the syndrome from which both Natasha and Nikolai are suffering. When Muratova first read his screenplay, 'I was interested in the subject of a man who falls asleep, tired out by everything in the world, not finding in himself the strength or energy or possibility to keep existing, to take part in this life: "I can't accept this world, I can neither fight it nor change it."'[10] Popov provided the short screenplay of the Natasha section, which he had written many years earlier. The literary excerpts Nikolai reads in the second part of the film were taken from Muratova's own diary: she called him, of all her heroes, the closest to herself.[11] 'People often assume that I wrote Natasha because she is a woman, and Sergei wrote Nikolai. In fact it's all intermixed. I'm very eclectic.'[12] The finished film diverges significantly from the officially approved shooting script. Muratova rearranged episodes, omitted some material entirely and added much that is new. But within episodes, the dialogue remains nearly identical with the shooting script, indicating that most of the changes came during editing.

The opening is abrupt: again there is no establishing shot, only a close-up of a broken and discarded doll covered with wilted flowers, prefiguring the flower-decked bodies we will shortly see in the cemetery. On the soundtrack, a haunting early string quartet by Schubert. Muratova contrasts the sublime beauty of Schubert's music with the physical and moral squalor she depicts. She chose Schubert because 'he's a very profound composer whose musical construction doesn't demand too much attention, doesn't distract from the image'.[13] Three old women, one grasping a large book (identified in the script as *War and Peace*), chant, not quite in unison: 'In my childhood, in my early youth, I thought it was enough for everyone to read carefully through the work of Lev Nikolaevich Tolstoy and everyone would understand absolutely everything. And everyone would become kind and intelligent.' There was originally only one old woman. By tripling her, Muratova used choral speaking to frame and emphasise their text, making it into the film's epigraph.[14] The women at once embody and gently parody the Russian intelligentsia's traditional view of the writer and of art's moral mission – a view continued in perverted form by Socialist Realism's notion of the writer as an 'engineer of human souls'.

> I could dedicate this film to Tolstoy. This is the key to my film. He says things about the naivety of the intelligentsia who believe that culture and art can transform the world...I believe that we can only draw attention, provoke, make people think, try to refine the soul and raise the mental level, but the essence of what is inside cannot be changed. This film is a tragedy consecrated to that fact.[15]

Muratova, however, is no cynical postmodernist; the old ladies' speech is a tacit confession that much of this traditional idealism remains in her own art. 'If I believed (*alas, I do not believe* [author's emphasis]) that art is capable of re-educating, of changing the world, then I, perhaps, would have given it [the sequence of profanity] up so that many people would have seen the film and been re-educated. But I'm not out to re-educate, I aim only to reflect.'[16]

Muratova did not undertake this long, psychologically exhausting film simply for pleasure, nor is that why she expects her audience to sit through it. There is a great deal of aesthetic pleasure to be had from *Asthenic Syndrome*, and much black humour, but it is inseparable from Muratova's moral orientation. Muratova wants to shock us with what she shows on the screen, for it is the everyday world in which we live, and we should be disturbed.

> For me there can be nothing more horrible than the scene in the dog pound, because of the universal human guilt towards creatures whom we have domesticated and who are innocent. Therefore, I don't find it as terrible to show the murder of one man by another. After all, the point is not to fill the screen with heaps of dead bodies, but to make some sort of essential statement about guilt and cruelty.[17]

She often speaks of the film's cathartic function. 'Every time I watch the episode with the queue for fish I experience a strange lightness, pleasure, liberation. Because I, like any woman, have often had to stand in such queues, and when I see that on the screen, it's as if I'm liberated from the oppressive, heavy feeling in life.'[18] But filming the scene at the dog pound did not bring the desired catharsis: 'I wake up and I think: the dogs we filmed have been butchered. They died a gruesome death, like in a death camp. And this is what we do to others and other animals.'[19] Throughout the film she used domestic animals – dogs, cats, even canaries – to provide a mute protest. Muratova, like the post-conversion Tolstoy, is a vegetarian. She attributed the turn that led her to make *Asthenic Syndrome* to 'the presence of Lev Tolstoy in my life, to his ideas and world-view...I so dislike the way nature and matter are arranged, how animals suffer, I don't like the fact that some of them eat others.'[20]

Only minutes into her film, Muratova confronts us with the aesthetic and moral grotesque that is to be her prime subject. She cuts from the old women to a small boy in an apartment window blowing bubbles, which have been floating across the screen since the opening frame. The idyllic image is a nod to Abuladze's *Repentance*, where the young girl Keti is blowing bubbles from the window of her apartment when she first sees the dictator Varlaam Aravidze. In *Asthenic Syndrome* the film's first appearance of evil also follows the bubble-blowing child, as Muratova cuts to a pit where construction workers are tying an empty can to the tail of a cat; others look on with amusement. Then she cuts to another pit – a fresh grave. An indifferent attendant, cigarette dangling from his mouth, directs hurried, assembly-line funerals. Hands arrange a drape around the body of a handsome middle-aged man. His hysterical widow Natasha utters an unearthly wail of primitive human grief, which breaks into the Schubert and silences it, then strides away through the cemetery, telling her friends: 'Go to hell, all of you.' These, her first words, shock by their contrast to her handsome, intelligent face and well-tailored suit. Julian Graffy has observed that this sequence intentionally echoes the cemetery

8. *Asthenic Syndrome*: Olga Antonova

setting at the opening of *The Long Farewell*, which the censors had found too gloomy.[21] Antonova's Natasha, like Sharko's Evgeniia, is a middle-aged blonde experiencing loss and transition. The closely spaced graves, surrounded, in the Russian manner, by wrought-iron fences, create a maze from which she tries to find an exit – a visual metaphor for her grief. A photograph of a stern older woman stares at her – and at us – from a gravestone. Muratova constructs a montage of such grave(n) images: faces of men, women, children – a panorama of Soviet reality. On the soundtrack there is total silence: no music to embellish these images or give us a clue as to how to read them. Leaving the cemetery, Natasha stands before another wall of sombre faces: the window of a photographer's studio displaying the standard ID shots that Soviet citizens needed for myriad documents.[22]

During Natasha's journey home from the cemetery, her ears (and ours) are assaulted by the shouts and abuse of the Soviet crowd – on the street, on public transportation. She responds in kind, then collapses in tears on a heap of rubbish, recalling the doll in the opening shot. Alone in her apartment, she sifts through pictures of herself and her husband in happier times. Muratova originally planned a flashback of Natasha and her husband together; the still photos are more effective in conveying the finality of his death. Natasha slides a wine glass to the edge of the piano, turns it upside down and, with no visible emotion, lets it drop. She stops by the hospital where she works and intentionally insults co-workers. On the street, the Schubert provides an incongruous counterpoint to her violent collisions with passers-by. Accosted by a lanky drunk (Sergei Chetverkov) she rejects his advances, then turns and peremptorily invites him home. With a doctor's impersonal tone she commands him to undress. He complies, in full view of the camera and, through the open apartment door, of a horrified neighbour. The nudity of his gaunt body is anti-erotic. In her bed she strokes and kisses him, then breaks into hysterical tears and throws him out.

Back on the street, a young woman tells Natasha she has a spot of whitewash on her coat. Such concern for the sartorial propriety of total strangers is common among Russian women. But this encounter is extended to exaggerated, and quite comic, length: the girl rubs at the spot with a handkerchief, reciting her words of solicitude as if reading from a script. We expect Natasha to lash out at her, too, notes Marina Topaz, but instead Natasha stands impassively as this segment ends.[23] The resigned gaze of suffering she addresses straight at the camera rhymes with the gaze of the doomed dogs in the film's culminating scene. A quick shot of the beam from a projector reveals that we have been watching a film within a film. In front of the screen, where the final frames are still rolling, strides an incongruously smiling pair: the actress who plays Natasha, and a genial master of ceremonies (Boris Vladimirsky).[24] This is to be a 'meeting with the audience', a common event in the Soviet Union, where local film clubs would meet to discuss a difficult or innovative film, often with the director present. The master of ceremonies urges the audience to stay, to 'discuss and ask questions, exchange impressions. We don't that often encounter really serious cinema.' They ignore him and rush for the exits, despite his increasingly desperate appeal: 'Real cinema, Aleksei German, Sokurov, Muratova.'[25] Vladimirsky comments: 'The actress and I are objects of [Muratova's] mordant irony. But it's also a self-irony. The self-irony of an artist who senses the powerlessness of the most masterful art before the enigma of artless reality.'[26] In the original script the audience was to learn early on that they were watching a film within a film – people are seen getting up and leaving in disgust. In Muratova's final version we do not discover this until the lights go up and the film switches to colour. The revision implicates us in her contention that there is little or no audience for 'serious' cinema such as hers. Any impatience that we, as viewers, have felt with the bizarre narrative we have been watching is caricatured by the reactions of the screen audience.

The shooting script highlights this moment of transition between black and white 'film' and full colour 'reality': 'The audience are in natural full colour...Everything suddenly seems very colourful, the wall, the bas-reliefs, the panelling, the chandeliers, the wall sconces, the vignette-like inscription about "the most important of the arts".' Muratova satirically, yet with compassion, predicts the response of the mass audience to her film. A middle-aged husband, by appearance a bureaucrat, complains to his wife:

> I don't understand why we have such sad films. I don't feel so good anyway. I'm tired out at work, I want to relax, listen to music, forget my troubles, look at something beautiful. But here they go again – walking around, whining, burying people, talking about all kinds of stuff.

Muratova's shooting script twice specifies a shot of 'an inscription about the most important of the arts'. The tongue-in-cheek reference is to the famous quotation attributed to Lenin, that 'the cinema is for us the most important of the arts', endlessly cited in Soviet film histories and once prominently displayed above the stage of Moscow's Dom Kino, the headquarters of the Film Maker's Union. Although the slogan itself does not appear in the final film, a large plaster bust of Lenin stands in for it. Under its blind eye, the master of ceremonies makes one last attempt to cajole the audience. Finally he grins, throws up his arms and, together with Antonova, dissolves in giggles. This moment has the look and feel of a take that Muratova kept precisely for its spontaneity. Only a detachment of Red Army soldiers remains in the hall. Their commanding officer barks orders to rise and leave, startling the sleeping Nikolai, the only other remaining member of the audience.

The subway at rush hour. Exhausted passengers, including Nikolai, sleep standing up, or meekly plod through crowded underground tunnels. As the supporting crowd disperses, he falls onto the platform. No one takes any notice; they simply step over him. The ambulance doctor called to the scene gives him a cursory examination. 'Is he drunk?' a policeman asks. 'No, he's simply asleep,' she replies, and begins to yawn, as does the policeman – Nikolai's narcolepsy is contagious. A Western spectator may need reassurance that this scene, like the previous one, evokes laughter of recognition in a Russian audience; sleeping drunks are such a common phenomenon in the Moscow subway that passers-by ignore them.

Late to class, Nikolai rushes down the school corridor. The vice-principal, a portly middle-aged blonde (Alexandra Svenskaia), polishes the glass on a wall exhibit of exemplary pupils. Nikolai tiptoes up the stairs, pausing in front of a kitschy stained-glass rendering of cats and other animals. Muratova zeroes in on the ugliness of Soviet public spaces: 'The corridor, like the entire school, is strongly and even garishly coloured...The decorative elements are even louder and larger than usual, or else our eyes, which have grown inured to bad taste, simply won't notice them.'[27] Nikolai finds temporary refuge in a lecture hall used for storage, full of now unneeded Lenin busts, and begins to recite a literary text. These are his first spoken words, and, like Valentina, Liuba and Maria in Muratova's earlier films, he begins by reciting a text rather than speaking spontaneously. Fittingly, his text speaks of the need constantly to utter the set speeches or scripts dictated to him by political and social norms, whether in his classroom, on the street, or even at home with his wife and mother-in-law. Like Muratova herself, Nikolai is all too painfully aware of the double-speak, unlike other characters in the film, who speak almost entirely in these clichés. Suddenly, his refuge is invaded by four women on the school staff, discussing the disappearance of a stray dog they have adopted. Muratova implicitly contrasts their concern for stray animals with the abuse they heap on their fellow humans: 'This was all Liushka the gardener's doing...You've got to go to Liushka and break her face.' Muratova particularly disliked the Soviet school, where the falsity of scripted discourse reaches its apogee:

Q: Is it accidental that your main hero works as a high-school teacher?
Muratova: Of course it's not accidental, because school is the first horror each of us confronts...Perhaps it's because I myself am a bad educator, but I hate school, simply hate it. When I enter any school I begin to sense something, 1 don't understand what – perhaps a certain smell, a sense of suffocation. I begin to talk with teachers – there's a kind of hypnotism of lying and mutual deception.[28]

She frames the scenes in Nikolai's classroom with sequences of moral anarchy in the world outside. In a memorable episode, Muratova films a shouting, pushing crowd and a harried, equally abusive fishmonger in one agonisingly long take of more than a minute and a half. A second shot moves imperceptibly closer and closer, as if we are waiting in a queue, to a close-up of the scale, the fish and the fish seller's hands in coarse gloves. The sound-track records the verbal abuse: 'Give me some clean ones!' 'You'll wash them at home!' 'I don't have running water at home!' Yet Muratova finds the scene somehow appealing.

> This scene could be filmed in a million ways – you could shoot it much more powerfully and crudely, but this is the way it is for me: horrible and at the same time cheerful, almost dancing along, as if they were all engaged in something pleasant... I find the queue terribly likeable because there's life in it... Well, you know, like Charlie Chaplin – a little man, everything seems to be going badly for him, but at the same time he feels good.[29]

She choreographs the transition from the fishmonger through a brief shot of another queue, this one to redeem glass jars and bottles, just below the window of Nikolai's classroom. Sound precedes image as we hear Nikolai's voice dictating, in English, from a textbook: 'In the future for our school graduates all roads are open: trade school, technicum, institute, university... Our school has achieved great success in its development.' Muratova's comment on this ideological drivel is oblique and visual: a sudden non-diegetic cut to a smoked fish lying on a table. The soundtrack plays a vintage recording of the old American popular song 'Chaquita', as young female fingers slowly rip the fish to pieces. In the classroom, the pupils are engaged in their usual occupations: drawing dirty pictures and daydreaming. Nikolai slips back into Russian: 'Man is friend, comrade and brother to man. This slogan is alien to the bourgeoisie.' Seating himself directly in front of Ivnikov (Pavel Polishchuk), a pupil who is staring out of the window at the belligerent glass redemption queue, Nikolai continues: 'Indifference is the characteristic trait of the bour-geoisie. The bourgeois is indifferent to the interests of society, to those around him... Ivnikov, I wonder what you see out there? Perhaps you'd like to share it with us?' 'I'm counting the bourgeoisie,' Ivnikov shoots back, revealing, in one pithy phrase, the hypocrisy of everything Nikolai has been saying. Nikolai suddenly begins to yawn, and retreats from the room.

Muratova cuts to a striking shot of his expressionless face framed between two stern photographs of model women workers on a plaque of honour. Their stolid faces recall the tombstone images, passport photographs and the model students on the corridor wall: Muratova estranges human images as well as human speech. Two girls are teasing a retarded man named Misha, but Ivnikov chases them away in front of a large poster proclaiming 'Our strength is in showing the truth – Lenin'. Nikolai is amazed that Ivnikov is actually acting in accordance with the altruism he himself has been preaching.

The next three episodes move from public to domestic spaces and end in family quarrels. Muratova's *mise en scène* and camera work highlight the cramped quarters in which ordinary Russians live – a pressure cooker for emotions. In each of the vignettes the central character eats alone, even though other family members are at home, symbolising the breakdown of human ties. A man enters his apartment, where his teenage daughter is dancing to music on the radio. He kisses her, she brings his slippers, he offers her an apple and begins to commune with his collection of caged canaries, which nearly fills the room. Suddenly the domestic idyll turns sour. A cat, incongruously wearing the red scarf of a Soviet pioneer, is draped over one of the cages. It reaches for a bird, the man chases it around the room, and the daughter comes to its defence, fighting and biting her father as he pulls her hair.

In the second vignette, Nikolai's mother-in-law (Natalia Ralleva) nags him about getting the floor repaired, making his own dinner, earning more money. He takes a jar of expensive black caviar out of the refrigerator; she puts it back with a meaningful look. If he is going to write, she asks, why cannot he be successful like his school friend who is already a member of a 'creative council'? (Those internal censorship bodies were the bane of Muratova's existence.) She reluctantly gives him permission to eat the caviar, and, staring at himself in the hall mirror, he eats it by the spoonful. Muratova explains:

> One doesn't eat caviar the way he does, gulping it down. He is surprised by it himself, he is in shock, he feels the need to look at himself in the mirror. He makes a spectacle of himself, he feels grandiose: he is in the middle of a performance. He must not even taste the caviar, so surprised is he by his own act. He hasn't written his novel, but he is eating caviar![30]

The sequence rhymes with the equally silent scene in Natasha's apartment, when, standing by the piano, she drinks water from a jar and eats bread: the act of eating, the heart of social interaction in Russian culture, has been made alien, devoid of pleasure and companionship.

At the dining room table Nikolai asks his wife Anna to open a third jar of caviar. The number three points to an important visual subtext, Andrei Rublev's icon of the 'Old Testament Trinity' (early fifteenth century), which depicts three angels seated at a table on which stands a footed bowl. Muratova mimics its composition in a long static shot of the table, with just such a footed bowl, where Nikolai sits facing the camera with his mother-in-law and wife. While we should be wary of attributing religious symbolism to Muratova's images (in more than one interview she has described herself as an unbeliever),[31] Christ-like imagery definitely surrounds the bearded, heavy-lidded Nikolai. His alienation from the world and his inappropriate behaviour in public spaces recall the Russian tradition of holy fools, venerated precisely for their kenoticism, or imitation of Christ. In a sense, Muratova's film, composed of loosely connected scenes, is itself like an iconostasis, the wall of icons mounted at the front of the church sanctuary. But her images are negative, anti-iconic, rather than positive. The trinity surrounding the table breaks into an ugly family quarrel.

Muratova probably rearranged the order of the three domestic vignettes (in the shooting script, Nikolai's scene came last) to end on a faint note of hope in the apartment of Irina Pavlovna, the portly vice-principal. In contrast to the stark drabness of the other two domestic spaces, hers is jammed with sentimental Soviet kitsch, which Muratova's camera studies in detail: paper flowers, paintings, plaster cupids, plastic kewpie dolls, crystal vases, tea sets. The silent soundtrack forces us to confront these images and make judgements without musical cues. The downstairs door opens with a clang, and we hear the mewing of kittens. Irina Pavlovna fondly abuses them in a high, rapid voice with a marked south Russian accent: 'Oh, you rotten little stinkers, you've certainly made yourselves at home.' Ivnikov, Nikolai's pupil, turns out to be her son. Despite the visual clues of dress and bearing that identify her

9. *Asthenic Syndrome*: Sergei Popov

as a typical 'Homo sovieticus', several reviewers note the shred of hope in this family, while there is none at all in Nikolai's. Muratova has commented, somewhat playfully, to an interviewer: 'I experience the tenderest sentiments towards my vice-principal. A character who is good to animals is, probably for that reason alone, sympathetic to the author.'[32] Sitting alone in the kitchen gulping soup and eating chocolates, Irina Pavlovna begins an exchange with her son in the same tone she used with the kittens: abuse is the way she expresses affection. Ivnikov leaves, but returns with a trumpet mouthpiece he has bought her. She begins playing 'Strangers in the Night', the title an ironic commentary on their relationship.[33]

Nikolai again dozes off in the next episodes, which juxtapose two bizarre gatherings – a young people's party and a teachers' meeting. Inside the apartment of his bohemian sister, a naked girl arranges herself, odalisque-like, on a sofa facing a mirror and a naked young man. Their nudity is not in the least erotic. Muratova explains:

> If you noticed, I accompanied this whole scene – a kind of theatricalized erotics or an erotic game that the young people have thought up – not with contemporary music, because that would inevitably convey for many the sense that this is evil, this is debauchery, but the music of Schubert. It should remind the audience that there exist old paintings where we see scenes depicting some sort of … picnic, *déjeuner sur l'herbe* … That's why I give them a *mise en scène* that recalls old masters: 'Venus and the Mirror', 'Venus and Cupid'. I underlie it with Schubert's beautiful music [the 'Unfinished' Symphony], which somehow makes it eternal and sublime.[34]

Nikolai falls asleep on the bed. A series of young men, totally nude and extremely serious, pose like models at a drawing class. The girl who originally posed with the hat stands nude and motionless for a very long take, staring at the camera, covering her genitals with her hands. The models' isolation, the artificial nature of their poses, and the total silence on the soundtrack strongly hint that this is Nikolai's dream (or nightmare). Mikhail Yampolsky points out that the scene is addressed directly to the audience as a 'poignant psychological provocation' by having the nudes stare directly at the viewer: 'a glance establishing an unambiguous contact between the naked body and the viewer has been invariably interpreted as pornography … Muratova denies the viewer the comfort of being an onlooker of the realities, she makes the viewer a component part of the grotesque picture she creates.'[35] Muratova is estranging pornography as she has already estranged the gaze and human speech, while returning to her initial Tolstoian question about the use, or misuse, of art.

From the 'obscenity' of the party we cut to the teachers' meeting, a satirical romp full of black humour. Nikolai sits at the back of the room, shaking himself violently to stay awake. Suddenly, his snoring attracts everyone's attention. Silence. Children, crowded behind glass-panelled doors outside the room, make grotesque faces, while animal noises play on the soundtrack. The children are then juxtaposed with the caged dogs of the following segment. The school secretary and her co-workers have come in search of their lost mascot. With cheerful naïvety they head for the holding cages, are horror-struck, and begin to cry. Music begins – a solo piano playing one of Schubert's 'Moments musicaux'. Several dogs huddle in a corner, too hungry, weak and ill even to bark. Muratova forces us to watch this for several very long takes, followed by a bare, black and white title in the didactic style of late Tolstoy:

PEOPLE DON'T LIKE TO LOOK AT THIS.
PEOPLE DON'T LIKE TO THINK ABOUT THIS.
THIS SHOULD HAVE NO RELATION
TO DISCUSSIONS OF GOOD AND EVIL.

For the second time in the film, Muratova directly addresses her audience. But, as the old ladies told us, reading Tolstoy is not enough. Even witnessing this inhumanity is not enough. Muratova has spoken obsessively of this scene in many interviews.

After this episode I have no other words. I gave them to one of my characters. But if I knew how to swear, that is the only thing that could succinctly and adequately be said after we see the dog pound. I didn't want to offend the audience, but there is a certain amount of provocation here. I wanted to turn us all around – myself included – and to prod us, to force us to keep our eyes open. If you don't like that, you have a right to be indignant. I don't like it either, that's why I show it.[36]

Why did she choose to use a title in this montage?

It's better to show something than to say it, but sometimes impossible: that's why I put the ironic title after the sequence with the dogs…The irony is to say, 'We are going to close our eyes, and speak of good and evil, to stop thinking about this.' But after this abominable dog pound, the chatter about man as 'the great creature' is demagogery. All words, all philosophy, are in vain.[37]

From the caged dogs, Muratova cuts to Nikolai, now himself imprisoned in a mental ward. A woman in a white coat closes the window and pulls the curtain. This would ordinarily signal that the next sequence is Nikolai's dream, but Muratova never makes things that easy: there is no corresponding signal that the dream has ended, and its action flows on into 'reality'. Nikolai's student Masha (Galina Zakhurdaeva) and her brunette friend (Natalia Buzko) have come to help him escape. In the shooting script, the sequence ends with what is still clearly a dream: they go out into virgin white snow and flee in a snowstorm, Masha's arms extended like wings as she rises in the air. But, in the film, there is only a statue of Ivan Pavlov (famous for his experiments with salivating dogs) bound in barbed wire in the hospital courtyard, followed by an abrupt cut to the infamous scene in the subway.

A woman in fashionable glasses and hat (Nadezhda Popova) sits in a subway car and speaks directly into the camera. '"Up your ass!" I say to him, and he says to me: "You prick!", and I answer him, "Fuck your mother, your father, your grandmother, your grandfather."' She enumerates other relatives, but the escalating sound of the train drowns her out. The young man next to her sleeps peacefully as her mouth clearly forms the words: 'Prostitute! Bastard! Cunt!' Elsewhere in the car, Masha and Nikolai gaze lovingly at each other, oblivious.

> I undertook *Asthenic Syndrome* in the hope of freeing myself from certain obsessive ideas and motifs, from my own gloomy state concerning this life. But I only dove once again into the horror of the existence of every living creature on this earth…That vulgar swearing at the end of the film…was a kind of 'political meeting' in the subway. After that I have nothing more to say.[38]

The much-discussed stream of vulgarity is uttered in an unreal tone, almost without affect. Yampolsky compares the episode to the earlier scenes of male nudity:

> Both scenes are energized by what I should call an 'inversion' mechanism. It is the female body that European culture has always regarded as a chief object of eroticism. The female body has traditionally posed as a less shocking, aestheticized object of delight and observation. Introducing a naked male as an object of observation breaks the standards of the European tradition…Making a woman instead of a man blurt out four-letter curses (as a verbal expression of degrading sexual aggressiveness) is another sign of this inversion of sexual roles in culture.[39]

Alexander Timofeevsky observes that the woman's stream of expletives rhymes with Natasha's despairing wail at the cemetery – another of the formal and thematic links in this long but meticulously structured picture.[40]

Masha and Nikolai are kissing like lovebirds. Nikolai leans back, seemingly in bliss…and falls asleep. When the train pulls into the last station, Masha tries frantically to wake him. A policeman walks through the empty cars. 'Is he dead?' he asks, recalling Nikolai's first subway scene. 'No, he's just asleep.' Masha flees the car as the lights go out and the train pulls out of the station. Nikolai falls off the seat, lying spread-eagled on the floor to a reprise of 'Chaquita'. He seems to be breathing, but looks more and more like the crucified Christ as the final titles roll.

The Odessa Studio submitted the finished film to Goskino on 5 October ·1989. On 15 October the Conflicts Commission of the Union of Film-makers issued its own resolution:

> One quality distinguishes Muratova's film from the many imitations filmed in the genre of 'chernukha': it is made with pain, it is permeated by pity for man, with all its brutality it doesn't humiliate either its heroes or its future audience. It would seem that the director works on the very edge of permissible frankness, but never,

not in a single shot, does she overstep the bounds... The Conflicts Commission doesn't consider it necessary or possible to correct this work in any way. The Commission takes Muratova's film under its protection because we are convinced that it is unique and in its way exceptional – and the shock therapy to which the director resorts is not an end in itself.[41]

Later that month Viktor Bozhovich, one of Muratova's long-time defenders, published a brief but strongly worded article about the still-unreleased film in the widely read *Moscow News*.[42] In mid-November Andrei Smirnov, acting secretary of the Union of Film-makers, organised a debate/press conference that included jurists, teachers and intellectuals. A member of the board of the State Censorship Commission [Glavlit] went on record with a remarkable statement testifying to the changed spirit of the times:

> I confine myself to a professional evaluation of this film, without addressing its high artistic merits. There are no revelations of state secrets, no open calls for overthrow of the present regime, and no pornography. Therefore, Glavlit has no objections to the release of the film. As for the last part of the film... this is a matter of taste and the desire of the director to express herself in the way she wishes. Though these expressions are 'unprintable', they have no relation whatsoever to the censorship.

A lawyer argued there was no basis for charging the film's creators under Article 206 of the criminal code on 'hooliganism', because they clearly were not 'intentionally uttering profanity with the aim of breaching public order'. Nevertheless, on 6 December Goskino gave permission for the film's release only on condition that the 'unprintable' expressions be removed.

On 10 December *Komsomolskaia pravda* published another article in the film's defence, quoting Muratova's assistant director, Nadezhda Popova, who, playing the woman on the subway, had uttered the words at issue. 'This is a return to prohibitions. To "the shelf". An infringement on the work of an artist.' The article concluded: 'Everyone understands that we have no stronger film today.'[43] On 15 December an official invitation to the Berlin Film Festival arrived by telex; a brief account of the brewing scandal appeared in the December issue of *Cahiers du cinéma* in Paris.[44] The affair quickly developed into an international embarrassment for Soviet officialdom. Goskino felt obliged to defend its decision. On 22 December *Komsomolskaia pravda* published a letter from its chairman, A.M. Kamshalov, who claimed the film had gone into production with no hindrance whatsoever, and additional funding was even provided when Muratova determined that the film would be longer than originally planned. 'We proceeded in this fashion because we were dealing with a master with a high creative reputation, and a screen play that promised to become a far from ordinary film. And we were not mistaken: *Asthenic Syndrome* is a real, great success for the director.' But, he continued, when

Goskino screened the film they found an unexpected episode.

> This episode (let's call it the episode in the subway) is entirely appropriate drama-
> tically, organically linked with the style of the film as a whole, but accompanied
> by such filthy language as, I swear, has never sounded from the screen in the
> entire history of our cinema. If this stream of unprintable abuse is preserved,
> it will be impossible to show the film not just to 'children under 16' but in any
> cinema where the audience is composed of people not alien to a sense of elementary
> decency.[45]

Still unreleased in the USSR, *Asthenic Syndrome* premiered on 19 February
1990 at the Berlin Film Festival, where it was awarded a Silver Bear. It was
entered in the festival not by Goskino, as was customary, but by the Odessa
Film Studio. According to Muratova, because of Goskino's refusal to send the
film a copy was sent out across the border with Lithuania, rather than through
Moscow, as was usual.[46] *Iskusstvo kino* reported on its Berlin reception:

> *Asthenic Syndrome* was received respectfully, and received the special prize of the
> jury. No one doubted the director's great cinematographic achievement – only, it
> seems, the film was not very well understood. Both the audience, many of whom
> did not sit through to the end, and the professional critics asked roughly the same
> questions: 'Is this...a kind of surrealism? An intentionally invented concentrate
> of unthinkable horror?' But no, this is a merciless look, cruel, but this is the way
> we live.[47]

Though the film had not yet been publicly shown in the USSR, rave reviews
began to appear in major Soviet publications.

> This picture is extraordinarily talented and kind-hearted...Perhaps it's one of the
> kindest films in our contemporary cinema, although, citing the soundtrack and
> describing two or three episodes, it would be easy to prove the opposite...The
> only chance to cure oneself of the asthenic syndrome is to wake up – to wake up
> and see the abyss into which we have fallen and try to climb out of it.[48]

'Finally in 1989 it has become clear what a director Kira Muratova could be if
they didn't get in her way.'[49] 'What is at issue, essentially, is the death of God.
God has died, and the entire second part of the film is already life after death.'[50]

After its debut in Berlin, *Asthenic Syndrome* was shown at the Créteil Festival
of Women's Films, the Quimper Festival in France, and the International
Festival of Women's Film and Video in Montreal. There were respectful reviews
in Western film journals.[51] 'It is difficult to think of a diagnosis of recent
Soviet experience that matches the clarity of Muratova's film or of an artist so
able to assess and reject her own previous methods, creating a new aesthetic
response to a new situation,' wrote Julian Graffy.[52] 'A wickedly humorous film
that seamlessly matches together the grotesquely theatrical with documentary
starkness...the product of an artistic imagination more akin to Fellini or
Makavejev,' commented J. Downie.[53]

After its success in Berlin the film was approved for release, not by Goskino but by the society of Friends of Film (the national organisation of film clubs) – an almost unprecedented situation – and approved for showings in film clubs and to those over sixteen. The society, and its president Irina Grashchenko, were given the responsibility to 'work with the film', preceding showings with talks by sociologists and film critics. *Asthenic Syndrome* finally premiered for a domestic audience at the Dom Kino in April 1990, and Goskino finally removed all bans on distribution in October. Soviet critics continued to praise and analyse the film, identifying its appearance as a major cultural/historical event. 'Muratova's greatest strength is her faultless ear for the…music of life…for the voice of the crowd, the intonations of the queue, the voices of its monsters and types…Muratova's cinema has the ability, in some magical way, to overcome horror and even somehow to make its peace with it.'[54] 'A film about "love" – the love of the author for her heroes. What stays with us is the image of an author who doesn't believe in the possibility of salvation and at the same time feverishly seeks it.'[55] In this authorial predicament lies the secret of *Asthenic Syndrome*'s continuing power. It is a timeless film, which continues to move and disturb audiences long after the Soviet apocalypse it so accurately foretold.

# 5. After Apocalypse

> *Asthenic Syndrome* is a film that has something of an impasse...I must now find
> another form and another content.
>
> Kira Muratova[1]

After *Asthenic Syndrome*, Muratova made two films much lighter in tone and
content. Each is full of her characteristic humour, sometimes gentle, sometimes not, about the absurdities of human existence.[2] Some critics, expecting
another moral-social diagnosis on the lines of *Asthenic Syndrome*, were puzzled
and disappointed. Muratova was annoyed when one described the characters of
*The Sentimental Policeman* as marionettes, moved by strings, and claimed she
had no sympathy for them. 'But the style of the film is normal primitivism,
primitivist drawings in which the characters are like the baby in their naivety.
This doesn't mean I don't love them. It means I adore them. The critics confuse
form with content.'[3]

There is a parallel to this shift in the work of Muratova's contemporary
Liudmila Petrushevskaia, whose writing Muratova greatly admires.[4] In early
1992 Petrushevskaia published *The Time: Night* [Vremia noch'], a bleak picture
of Russian family life. Like *Asthenic Syndrome*, it is a masterpiece that some
critics labelled 'blackening of reality' (*chernukha*). But in the first post-Soviet
years Petrushevskaia also published a large number of fairly tales (*skazki*) 'for
grown-ups' or 'for the whole family', clever and playful updatings of traditional
fairly-tale motifs with happy endings. A new era had arrived, but life was still
hard. Muratova, Petrushevskaia and their audiences had enough dark critiques
of Soviet society, and looked for hope, albeit tempered with wry humour, in
post-Soviet fairy tales.

*Enthusiasms*, in Muratova's words, is 'a chamber film, which avoids the sad
sides of life...It was conceived and done that way...A girl wants to be a circus

performer, but it's not working out... Well, that's not a tragedy.'[5] Along with
*The Sentimental Policeman*, *Enthusiasms* continued Muratova's examination of
the proposition that 'no one loves anyone'. A film full of beautiful people,
horses, and landscapes, it may be, as Muratova warned her audience, 'a light,
"salon" film, absolutely superficial', but it also is a film in which, obsessed by
their enthusiasms, no one loves anyone else.

These were the first films in which Muratova had to deal with the new
post-communist realities of film production. Initially she was philosophical,
and even realistic, about the prospect:

> What has begun is the dependence on money, on the public. But I believe these are
> natural difficulties while the ideological difficulties were not... There are temptations
> coming from the West. Before, my crew and my actors wanted to work with me at
> any cost. It didn't depend on their salaries because they were very badly paid, so
> a bit more or less didn't make any difference. Now, they can say to me: 'You know,
> I love you, it's fabulous to work with you, but I have a family, children, and I want
> to earn some money.'[6]

*The Sentimental Policeman*, her first and only experience with international co-
production, was, however, a disaster from her point of view. 'I was seduced and
abandoned... It's not normal when they come here as if to an undeveloped
colony.'[7] A friend of Muratova's who acted in the film as a non-professional
described conditions of demoralisation and irresponsibility on the set – all too
typical in the immediate post-Soviet film industry and post-Soviet society as
a whole. Muratova's assistants were more interested in flirting and drinking
with the French film crew than in doing their jobs, and she was left to do the
bulk of the work by herself.[8] Her experience with the 'New Russian' million-
aires who promised financing for *Enthusiasms* was little better, as one by one
they went bankrupt in the chaotic first years of the post-Soviet economy.

### *The Sentimental Policeman* [1992]

> Often, when I met with the audiences of *Asthenic Syndrome*, very many of them,
> particularly the women, simply said to me in tears that this was impossible and
> they needed something to console them.

Kira Muratova[9]

*The Sentimental Policeman* continued Muratova's investigation of intimate human
relationships. She intended the film as an assertion that life and love will and
must go on even after the Soviet apocalypse. It is an eccentric comedy, full of
the sight gags that animated the silent comedies Muratova loves. Her hero,
Officer Tolia Kiriliuk, is Chaplinesque; the film reminded French reviewers of
Jacques Tati.[10] Muratova described it as 'the polar opposite of *Asthenic Syndrome*

in all respects. I'm always drawn from the sweet to the sour. This is a small, closed, chamber tale and very sentimental. Perhaps there are echoes of *Getting to Know the Big, Wide World*.'[11] The plot could not be more different from *Asthenic Syndrome*: a young policeman (Nikolai Shatokhin) finds an abandoned baby in a cabbage patch (yes, a cabbage patch!), and by the time he has carried her to the police station and then to the children's home he has become attached to her. He and his wife Klava (Irina Kovalenko) decide to adopt the baby, but she has already been promised to a widowed, middle-aged paediatrician, Dr Elena Zakharova (Natalia Ralleva). They appeal against the decision in court, but lose when Zakharova produces as evidence the model son she adopted as a baby. After the trial, Klava confesses to Tolia that she is pregnant.

The original idea came from a real incident: Muratova read a sketch by Odessa journalist Yuri Usichenko about a court case over custody. She wrote the screenplay during the period in the 1970s when she was not allowed to direct, then proposed the idea to Soviet television, but it was squelched because 'in our country there are no abandoned children'. Muratova had just begun shooting *The Sentimental Policeman* in Belgorod-Dnestrovsky, a town on the Black Sea south of Odessa, when the 19 August 1991 putsch signalled the final death throes of the Soviet Union. She set off in the morning with her

10. *The Sentimental Policeman*: Nikolai Shatokhin

Russian crew and French co-production staff, and was terribly upset when, instead of working, everyone was glued to a portable television. 'What's there to watch?' she said. 'Yanaevs [Gennadi Yanaev, Soviet Vice-President, was one of the conspirators] come and go, but nevertheless we've got to work, even today.'[12] *The Sentimental Policeman* became one of the very first post-Soviet films.

While her three previous films had been dominated by death, *The Sentimental Policeman* is again about love. After the film's premiere in February 1992 at Moscow's Kino Centre, Muratova assured journalists that this was a 'sincere and naive story...almost a fairy tale', and defined its aesthetic as 'something close to the shop window of an Odessa photo studio, where rosy-cheeked babies and smiling newly-weds goggle at you...'[13] When they preferred to discuss the degradation of society and the degeneration of humanity, she exclaimed: 'Humanity? Society? Oh, leave me alone! The only thing real and beautiful in this world is one or another form of love, the babe in the arms of Mary or Joseph.'[14] Muratova provided at least two clues that the film is, in some ways, a nativity tale. One is the phrase about the babe in the arms of Joseph, which she put in the mouth of the eccentric owner of the cabbage patch; the other is the music she chose to accompany the long opening sequence – the twelfth of the pieces in Tchaikovsky's piano suite *The Seasons*, titled 'Sviatki' (Noël/Christmas).

The film is full of hopeful answers to *Asthenic Syndrome*. The young policeman and his wife, the kindly Dr Zakharova and the adorable, un-believably calm baby Natasha belong stylistically as well as morally to a fairy-tale world entirely alien to the hostility and indifference that surround them. In the opening shot of *Asthenic Syndrome*, a naked doll lay forlornly with withered flowers on a rubbish heap. *The Sentimental Policeman* opens with a smiling baby, also naked, surrounded by huge cabbages. Officer Kiriliuk is seated in profile in the classic pose of Rodin's *Thinker*, with a broken plastic doll in his hand. An overhead shot cuts back to Natasha, equally naked, her genital area covered by a discreetly placed cabbage leaf. As Kiriliuk tries to repair the doll, he will also try to put Natasha's life back together. Muratova saw him as 'a person who wants to bring order into the life of one very small being'.[15] Like Chaplin's tramp, Tolia Kiriliuk is naïve, but far from stupid. The baby's cry breaks into Tchaikovsky's music and silences it, echoing the older Natasha's wail at the cemetery in the first part of *Asthenic Syndrome*, which silenced the music of Schubert. Several actors from *Asthenic Syndrome* reappear in the new film. Natasha, namesake of *Asthenic Syndrome*'s widowed doctor, is given to another widowed doctor, played by the actress who portrayed Nikolai's carping mother-in-law. The memorable Alexandra Svenskaia, who played the harridan vice-principal, turns up as a staff member at the children's home. But a reference to *Asthenic Syndrome*'s caged dogs is not so optimistic: an unwatched television screen in Dr Zakharova's apartment shows a documentary of stray dogs being captured and carted off to the pound.

Tolia's relationship with Natasha becomes an island of compassion in a world where people constantly scream at each other and human interaction in public spaces and institutions (the street, the police station, the orphanage, the courtroom) is grotesque and meaningless. He bends over her, puzzled, then, in a sudden rush of inspiration, removes his shirt and wraps it around her. This will be a moment of revelation for him: 'I covered her with my shirt, and she stopped crying,' he later repeats, vainly expecting others to understand the cosmic significance of this simple human event. But, despite Muratova's assurances about the film's simplicity, reviewers immediately sensed a disjunction between its anecdotal, sentimental plot and its mannered style. They noted the film's stylistic relationship both to Socialist Realism (the conflict between 'the good and the still better') and to the artistic movement of 'sots-art', which recycled the style of Socialist Realism in postmodernist parody. Several pointed out that the figure of the Soviet policeman (*militsioner*) was central to a series of 'graphomanic' poems penned by Dmitri Prigov, the prime exemplar of sots-art in Russian poetry.[16] Indeed, Klava complains to Tolia about 'all those jokes about policemen'.

Lev Anninsky, a cultural critic from the generation of the 1960s, sought a deeper socio-political meaning:

> There's no water in the taps, there's rubbish and garbage in the courtyards, there's nothing to eat, mothers abandon their babies, who lie and wait till they are 'found' – is this order? The authorities have fallen away, the government has no money for anything, homeless dogs roam the streets... Where can you call, whom can you summon, to whom can you complain?

To him, the film was simply an elaboration of the diagnosis Muratova had made in *Asthenic Syndrome*.[17]

Actually, *The Sentimental Policeman* is less concerned with sots-art than with paying homage to the artistic experiments of the early Soviet avant-garde. *The Sentimental Policeman*'s opening sequence is, in effect, a silent film. The colour palette is close to black and white (it was probably filmed with a blue filter to simulate night-time). Until Natasha's cry breaks in, we hear only a solo piano, like the accompaniment in silent movie theatres. The long takes recall the pre-Revolutionary melodramas, before the montage school introduced rapid cutting; Tolia's mechanistic movements echo theatre director Meyerhold's biomechanical acting style, which strongly influenced the avant-garde filmmakers of the 1920s. That heritage is particularly clear when Kiriliuk performs a strange leaping dance around the cabbage patch searching for the unseen baby. His exaggerated 'eccentric' movements recall those of Andrei Kostrichkin as Akaki Akakievich in Kozintsev and Trauberg's *The Overcoat* [1926], a production informed by Russian formalist Boris Eikhenbaum's analysis of Gogol's classic story, 'How Gogol's Overcoat Was Made'. In that seminal study, Eikhenbaum analyses the disconnect between the story's 'pathetic' content and the way Gogol distances the reader through the crafty use of an unsophisticated narrator. Viktor Matizen has noted the similarity in Muratova's film:

> The contradiction between the sentimental plot and the author's totally unsentimental gaze is the main conflict of the film, and constitutes its greatest interest... I don't know whether Muratova studied Eikhenbaum's 'How Gogol's Overcoat Was Made', but the overcoat of her *Sentimental Policeman* is made to the measure of the formalist school.[18]

Tatiana Moskvina describes 'the picturesque primitivism of Muratova's crafty language' as 'a sort of kino-mask, analagous to literary masks', and the film's theme as 'how many good-hearted idealists and kind fools were born in the Soviet dormitory, where the ideologues of collectivism and self-sacrifice found their knights and martyrs'.[19]

*The Sentimental Policeman* also pays homage to the early Eisenstein. A long shot of Tolia's hand rotating in movements that recall Meyerhold's bio-mechanical études has no clear diegetic meaning. It is not unlike Paradjanov's abstract joy in the visual, but could also be described in Eisenstein's term as an 'attraction'.[20] When Tolia puts his ear to the ground, the triple repetition

11. *The Sentimental Policeman*: Andrei Kasianov, Leonid Kushnir, Ekaterina Lobanova (photo credit: E. Golubenko)

mimics Eisenstein's 'expansion of action' famously embodied in the sequence of the sailor breaking the plate in *Battleship Potemkin*. A shot of two zoo lions yawning follows one of Tolia and Klava yawning, gently parodying *Potemkin*'s 'awakened' stone lions. Much has been written about Eisenstein's use of small children as innocent victims of tsarist oppression. Muratova chose the Odessa steps, site of *Potemkin*'s Cossacks and descending baby carriage, for a very different scene: Tolia the policeman confesses to his wife that he wants to adopt a baby. They embrace in the middle of the staircase, just where in *Potemkin* a distraught mother stood with her dying son, pleading with the Cossacks for mercy. A ray of light casts their shadow on the steps, recalling the unmotivated ray of light behind Eisenstein's mother as she carries her son, pietà-fashion, back up the steps.[21]

There are visual quotations of Constructivist icons as well: Katerina Clark has noted the two posters of Kazimir Malevich's black square that decorate the walls of Kiriliuk's apartment, and the draped statue atop the Odessa steps, recalling Natan Altman's decorations for Petrograd's Palace Square in celebration of the first anniversary of the October Revolution.[22] The camera focuses on a cracked cement wall by the steps, and Tolia makes a statement of faith: 'I look at that wall, and the crack, and the grass, and the bush. It's as if I love it and I feel sorry for it. All the rest is like death, everything that's not love.' The light changes and the camera dollies back to reveal that the crack is now an abstract painting in an elaborate frame – a transformation of ugliness into art, and perhaps a playful reference to the Constructivist slogan 'Life into Art!'

From the fairy-tale world of the opening sequence, where broken dolls can be repaired and babies found in cabbage patches instantly comforted, Muratova cuts to a cacophony of leashed dogs barking viciously on a nearby street. Shirtless, and (like Joseph) with the babe in his arms, Tolia sits on a bench watching the spectacle. Neighbours at their balcony windows create a kind of Greek chorus – 'politely, in Odessa fashion,' one reviewer jokingly phrased it. Their ritualised, rhythmic insults are the human equivalent of the territorial barking below, creating a grand fugue in which words are arranged into meaningful sentences, but the entire sequence is devoid of meaning.

> Take away those dogs! They don't let us sleep!
> They raise dogs, they fatten them up, while people have nothing to eat!
> ...
> Take them to the dog pound! To the knacker's yard!
> You're a fascist! It's you who are a fascist!
> ...
> Bastards! First they tame them, and then...
> The dog is a friend to man...
> Tell me, is your dog also a Yid?
> ...

Tell me, is your dog also a Jew?
I'm a Jew, nowadays that's prestigious, and she's a Jewess.
Drop dead, you dirty Jew!

At the end of the sequence, a woman in red sadly repeats, 'The dog is a friend to man. First they tame them, then...' Both the actress and her words reprise *Asthenic Syndrome*; she played the secretary to the school director and, invoking that slogan, organised the rescue expedition to the dog pound. The scene is a masterpiece of visual and aural montage: Muratova's defence against the world's ugliness is to transform it into art.

Clark has analysed the film's intentionally unnatural use of language.

> Throughout, Muratova draws attention to its essentially staged nature, its 'theatricality'. The hero, in recounting his most intense experiences, recurrently uses expressions meaning 'as if...'. There are unmotivated vignettes of fatuous declamation and hyperbolically theatrical stylization, gratuitous repetitions, motivated, if at all, by their different inflections, jerky, sudden transitions from one acting style to another, and dialogues that are exercises in non-communication, some somewhat Pinteresque, others more Gogolian.[23]

The repetition of phrases and gestures is more pronounced in *The Sentimental Policeman* than in Muratova's previous films. Doubling – of characters, actions and spoken lines – is an important element in the film's style, even, Boris Kuzminskii has argued, a basic device of its construction.[24] Natasha has two equally good claimants to adopt her; in the children's home the attendants speak in pairs, slightly out of synch; and there are two workers in the yard – one missing a left hand, one a right. There are two black squares on the wall of Tolia and Klava's bedroom, and as the couple wakes up in the morning they go through their morning ritual – dressing, tying their shoes – in parallel. We witness that ritual not once but twice. The baby even has an incongruous double in a homeless man who seeks shelter in the police station. The grey-haired eccentric explains: 'Mama doesn't let me back into the house after 11 p.m.,' repeating the sentence nine times, varying the intonation and word order, convincing us of its falsehood, as Kiriliuk listens, impassive and annoyed. These two 'abandoned children' look to Kiriliuk, bemused representative of a dissolving state, to bring shelter and order into their lives. While he stands motionless and uncertain, a more confident mother figure enters the station: Dr Zakharova has been summoned to examine the foundling. The stylistics of comic chaos instantly vanish as the calm, competent physician examines the cooing baby.

Tolia and Klava wake in their new, sparsely furnished apartment, nude and innocent like Adam and Eve – and Natasha. The water has been shut off (nearly twenty-five years after *Brief Encounters*, Muratova reminds us, Odessa still had water supply problems), and they wash by pouring buckets of cold water over each other, drying themselves with a shared towel. Critics have tried to explain the asexuality of their morning nudity by assuming it symbolises the sterility of their era or of their marriage.[25] But Muratova says of Tolia, 'He's married, young, handsome, he has no problems in having his own children'.[26] It may simply be that this naive fairy-tale hero has not yet thought seriously about how babies are made – hence the opening scene in the cabbage patch. Waxing philosophical as they dress for work, he tries to convince Klava that their own meeting was 'by chance', and could just as well have never taken place.[27] Klava was raised in a children's home, and having taken in one orphan he thinks he is destined to adopt another. Klava's assent – 'Let's adopt her' – is another occasion for doubling (and humour), since Tolia uses the Russian word for 'adopt', which literally means 'to make a son of' (*usynovit'*). Klava keeps correcting him, using the parallel form, 'to make a daughter of [*udocherit'*]'.

Like the other institutions of state power in the film, the police station and the courtroom, the children's home is depicted in the mode of the absurd. It is quarantined because of scarlet fever and under renovation – perhaps a sly metaphor for the political crisis taking place as the film was being shot. Tolia and Klava arrive with character references and the proper paperwork, but are met by the staff with evasion. In the courtroom, the mood is truly Gogolian: absurdity reigns. Their lawyer's speech is interrupted by a loud ship horn from the neighbouring dock; the door refuses to stay closed; the judge seems oblivious of both the law and the case; the clerk has the features of a kewpie doll. Muratova is fond of filming the physically 'different'.

Muratova did not originally intend to use any music. 'The film is already very sentimental, it seems to me that it will be very sweet. [Music] will repeat those same feelings that I already had. Because *Asthenic Syndrome* is a tough, hard film, that's why the music in it is beautiful, as a kind of counterpoint, but in this film I want to do without music, because with music there's sometimes a kind of "painting over" or some kind of palliative.'[28] But she did eventually use music, though sparingly. Three excerpts from Tchaikovsky's *The Seasons* are associated with Natasha and those who want to adopt her: 'Sviatki/Noël' when Tolia discovers the baby, 'March: Song of the Swallow' as Zakharova walks home after examining her, and 'October: Song of Autumn' during the scene on the Odessa steps. At the end of the film, chansonnier Alexander Vertinsky's melancholy 'Alien Cities' plays over a long scene of a father trying to juggle a toddler, a shopping bag and a chicken, while the credits roll. Vertinsky's lyrics, and the predicament of the lone father, temper the sweetness of Klava's confession of pregnancy: 'The people here are alien, with alien joys and sorrows, and we will be alien for them for ever.'[29]

After an invitational screening at the Moscow Kino Centre in February 1992, reviews began to appear in the Moscow press.[30] The film premiered on

16 April. At the 1992 Kinotavr Festival in Sochi it won the prize in the category 'Films for the Select Few'. It was shown at the Venice Film Festival that summer, and at the Créteil Festival in April 1993. Muratova complained that there were invitations to a number of other festivals, but Paris-Media, the French co-producers who owned the negative, didn't take the trouble to print copies in time.[31]

## *Enthusiasms* [1994]

Every person born, even if not attractive, always experiences in his life a peak of beauty.

Lilia – *Enthusiasms*

*Enthusiasms* won Muratova the 1994 Nika award for best Russian director. When it premiered at the 1994 Berlin Film Festival, Muratova warned: 'Don't expect another *Asthenic Syndrome*. The film you are about to see is a light, "salon" film, absolutely superficial. Take it for what it is, or leave the hall and don't waste your time.'[32] She was once again provoking her audience, but in the opposite direction. In *Asthenic Syndrome* she forced the spectator to confront the moral and aesthetic ugliness of late Soviet society. Now, in the first post-Soviet years of economic, social and artistic turmoil, Muratova threw her audience and critics another challenge: here is a film that you will love to look at, but it has no significant message – it exists to please me and those who love the beautiful. In place of starving, flea-bitten dogs and tormented cats, her camera focuses on exquisite, thoroughbred racehorses in motion, handsome jockeys, and two beautiful women with the flower names of Violetta and Lilia, amidst some of the most spectacular scenery in Russia. There had always been much to please the eye in Muratova's films. But, in the earlier work, this was because she found new and interesting perspectives to film the everyday. In *Enthusiasms*, her camera does not have to produce beauty – just capture it. 'To what purpose?' Russian critics asked. 'To none at all, except pleasure,' Muratova seems to answer. *Enthusiasms* is one of Muratova's most beautiful films, and one of her most amusing, if we are attuned to her offbeat sense of humour.

*Enthusiasms*, like *The Sentimental Policeman*, was based on screenplay Muratova wrote in the mid-1970s. Radomir Vasilevsky, a fellow Odessa director, asked her to write a script about horses and horse racing. Though she herself is afraid of horses and doesn't ride, Muratova read up on the subject and produced a screenplay based on the stories of the horseman Boris Dediukhin. But Vasilevsky didn't like it, and it lay fallow for years.[33] She decided to film it herself, shooting with her favourite cameraman, Gennadi Kariuk, on the shore of the Black Sea and at the world-famous stud farm in Piatigorsk, at the foot of the Caucasus Mountains. The film's title has been translated variously as 'Obsessions', 'Passions' and 'Avocations'. The Russian original describes something that draws a person towards itself and away from other interests. In the context of the film, it refers to the jockeys and their obsession with racing, Lilia and her obsession with death, Volodia the photographer and his retouched photos of 'centaurs'. The characters' lack of attachment to each other is mirrored in the film's intentional aloofness from its own audience – their enthusiasms leave no room for human relationships. 'I became entranced with the very style of this world, the thought of how many separate "worldlets" of all sorts exist, which are completely forgotten, exist in isolation and aren't interested in any criteria of the outside other world.'[34] What motivated Muratova was her passion for studying the human animal, rather than conveying a message. She has hinted that there was an element of self-analysis in this study: 'Everyone is carried away by his own thing, and that enthusiasm pushes the rest of the world into the background. I am carried away by cinema – just as horsemen are by their world.'[35]

*Enthusiasms* is famous as the film in which Muratova discovered the acting talent of screenwriter Renata Litvinova, who won a Nika for her role as Lilia.

12. *Enthusiams*: Svetlana Kolenda, Renata Litvinova, Alexei Shevchenko, Umirzak Shmanov, Mikhail Demidov (photo credit: E. Golubenko)

*Enthusiasms* and *Three Stories* are illuminated – some might say dominated – by her presence. Litvinova, daughter of two Moscow physicians, graduated from the screenwriting faculty of VGIK in 1989. She was already something of a celebrity in Moscow's New Russian society by the early 1990s for her screenplays, as well as her striking self-image, which she styled after the legendary fatal blondes of cinema history – Jean Harlow, Marlene Dietrich, Greta Garbo and Marilyn Monroe. She has been the subject of numerous profiles in the Russian press, and played Constance Bulitsky in Peter Greenaway's *The Tulse Luper Suitcases, Episode 3: Antwerp* [2003]. Tatiana Moskvina has compared Litvinova's 'mythic' role in the 1990s to that of poetess Bella Akhmadullina in the 1960s: 'A combination of talent, beauty, presence in society, a stormy personal life and early fame.'[36]

Muratova first met Litvinova at the Arsenal Film Festival in Riga some years before she began work on *Enthusiasms*. 'I had read her screenplay "A Principled and Compassionate Gaze" ... I went up to her to say how much I liked it. I saw her and I thought: "I could film her as well! She tells such stories, she's so beautiful. That is unique." In general, I'm not interested in beauties, but she's a distinctive beauty. She's an eccentric.'[37] She invited Litvinova to try out for the role of Violetta, the circus performer. But her appearance was clearly inappropriate: 'The circus performer has to be a princess, and Renata is a queen. But I was so anxious not to lose her that the heroine was doubled.'[38] Muratova had done that before with the twins in *Getting to Know the Big, Wide World* and the school pupils in *Asthenic Syndrome*. 'Doubling, doubles – is strikingly interesting. It seems to me that there's a very ancient curiosity about doubling in nature.'[39] Plakhov has hypothesised that Violetta (Svetlana Kolenda) represents Eros, while Litvinova's Lilia represents Thanatos. 'For Muratova, as for Freud, these two – love and death – are interdependent.'[40]

It is probably more than coincidental that Litvinova, the daughter of physicians, directed by Muratova, also the daughter of a physician, plays a nurse in this film and a maternity home archivist in *Three Stories*. It was Golubenko who first suggested making her character a nurse, since the opening scenes take place at a hospital. Litvinova agreed, but did not want her character to be in love with anyone. They began with only a first line: 'The morgue – it's good. The morgue – it's cool, chilly.' Then Litvinova proposed some monologues she had already written. Muratova chose appropriate ones, 'and then her character grew and took over the central position in comparison with the circus performer, who had been the more important. That is, she pushed her aside.'[41]

The film's opening shots are filled with the saturated colours of green grass, white nurses' uniforms, blue sea and sky, Violetta's multicoloured flower garland and her circus make-up – vivid red mouth against clown-white skin – as Muratova moved beyond ornamentalism to a new simplicity in the use of colour.[42] Violetta, the third generation of a matriarchal circus family, is recuperating from a broken leg at a seaside sanatorium. Sasha Milashevsky (Alexei Shevchenko), a jockey, has far more serious job-related injuries: 'multiple trauma, internal bleeding, ribs…' he cheerfully enumerates from the wheelchair to which he is confined, immobilised by casts on both legs and both arms. None of this dampens the ebullient mood of the opening sequence, in which his fellow jockeys, Sania Kasianov (Mikhail Demidov) and Nars Narkisov (Umirzak Shmanov), have come to visit him. The choral movement of Beethoven's Ninth Symphony rises on the soundtrack as the film cuts to a long sequence of two middle-aged men engaged in friendly horseplay on the beach. The overwhelming mood is that of the choral text, 'Ode to Joy': the jockeys, Violetta and the men on the beach are revelling in the beauty of the scenery and the weather. It is a rare mood for Muratova, and that should make us suspect its role as a thematic statement, to which the rest of the film will give a nuanced reply. Plakhov has sagely observed:

> Muratova herself meticulously puts every substance to the test. In *Brief Encounters*, it was the romanticism of distant roads, in *The Long Farewell* – exalted maternal sentiments, in *The Sentimental Policeman* – the healthy instinct for continuation of the human race. And each time it turns out that there is a limit to everything, and that beyond this limit the result is the destruction of the material, collapse/disintegration, a yawning black hole.[43]

In fact, the 'Ode to Joy' undermines itself from the outset. Since World War II this music has carried an association with Nazism for Russians of an older generation.[44] Abuladze used it, memorably, in *Repentance* as a tragic counterpoint to the torture and killing of his Christ-like artist-hero, Sandro Baratelli.

As Lilia, a sexy blonde vamp in a nurse's uniform, Litvinova performs morbid monologues about the morgue, her dead friend Rita Gauthier,[45] and a sixteen-year-old who hanged himself for unrequited love. When Violetta tries to persuade Milashevsky to join the circus, Lilia counters with the alternative of becoming an orderly, and carrying jars of organs around. The comic twist is that no one responds in any way to her monologues. Violetta, uninhibited by the cast on her leg, performs a dance and twirling routine with her cane. In a deadpan sequence that again reveals Muratova's fondness for silent comedy, four young female patients in bathrobes observe Violetta and, one by one, like a series of puppets, come alive with imitative dance movements.

Kasianov invites the girls to the hippodrome, and Violetta confesses to Lilia that she is looking for a partner for a new equestrian act. In the horse barn, Violetta, in a black cape, and Lilia, in a slinky, sequined black dress, both in black high-heeled pumps, are looking for attention. Their graceful pacing movements parallel those of the horses. But the men are consumed by their passion for horseflesh and indifferent to female beauty. Lilia strikes poses for Volodia, but he is simply gesturing her out of the way, trying to photograph a horse behind her. In a long sequence of more than a minute, beautiful horses pace in their stalls, staring soulfully back at the camera, with only their whinnying on the sound track. Oleg Nikolaev, an amateur jockey, passes Violetta and observes, 'That's a very attractive girl' – literally 'a bestially beautiful girl' (*zverski krasiviaia devushka*). The adverb is telling – Nikolaev and his companions evaluate Violetta's supple form the way they would admire a fine horse. Lilia observes to a stable-boy, 'It's so dirty here. I want to leave. I'm going to leave.' 'So leave!' he retorts. But Lilia can't bring herself to leave without someone noticing her exit: she poses and paces in a brilliant imitation of equine movement. In Litvinova, Muratova discovered a talented comic actress not unlike Marilyn Monroe.[46]

When an interviewer characterised this film as 'the first in which you investigate the theme of the male and female principle through your young heroes,' Muratova replied heatedly, 'This is in every one of my films.'[47] The film's love triangles are unconventional and unstable. Kasianov flirts with Violetta, who in turn courts him as a potential partner. Amirov, the local trainer, courts Kasianov, urging him to join him and ride his horses. Kasianov's trainer (Popov) plots to fix a race against Amirov. Nikolaev looks meaningfully at what we assume is Violetta, but the next shot reveals he has been looking at Kasianov, or – more likely – Kasianov's horse. The two challenge each other to a race over Violetta, but Nikolaev reconsiders. 'Why involve the horses? Horses are above all that.'

Plakhov sees an 'unintentional travesty' of *Asthenic Syndrome* in the film's only sequence set in the circus, where Violetta's mother is training cats and dogs. 'Now the dog cage has taken on the circular form of the circus arena, and the trainer tirelessly, with the stubbornness of a parrot, repeats that she "doesn't beat, doesn't beat, doesn't beat…" her charges.'[48] At this point, Violetta's grandmother erupts in a phrase worthy of *Asthenic Syndrome*'s woman on the subway. Then Svenskaia, who played the trumpet-playing vice-principal, descends to the ring in a swing, dressed as a grotesque Fellini-esque clown, playing an accordion. These unexplained elements seem to support Plakhov's argument that this episode is related to *Asthenic Syndrome*, but, ironic self-quotation aside, it is not entirely clear how or why.

Shooting was interrupted several times for lack of money. But then Litvinova, whom Muratova called the good angel of the film, found producer Igor Kalenov.[49] It premiered at the 1994 Berliniale, in the non-competition programme. On 4 March 1994 there was a packed press screening at the Moscow Kino Centre, followed by a cluster of reviews in Moscow newspapers.

Plakhov commented: 'That which in her work was once tragedy (or provincial melodrama) now returns in the guise of absurd comedy ... This is a light and totally innocent film.'[50] *Nezavisimaia gazeta* reported that for the first twenty minutes or so the audience of curious journalists 'chuckled in a friendly manner, but the rest of the time only Muratova's fans watched the film with undisguised interest, while the other parts of the hall snored rhythmically ... Kira Georgievna has made a very nice and very boring film.'[51] Another critic defined the film's genre as 'an unusual mixture of the radiant absurd and the melodramatic farce ... The latest strange poem of an artist who doesn't intend to teach anyone anything.'[52] V. Turovsky voiced his now habitual complaint. 'One of our most talented directors long ago stopped loving her heroes, sympathizing with them, admiring them. It's as if she's taking revenge on her new characters for all the pain she herself experienced and overcame.' He grudgingly subtitled his review 'Every film of Kira Muratova is worthy of attention. Even this one.'[53] The ever-sympathetic Bozhovich suggested a reason for the film's lack of human warmth: 'Totally unconcerned about being "contemporary", Kira Muratova possesses the unique ability to capture the spirit and tendency of the time.'[54] Bykov wrote: 'Muratova is remarkable in that plot doesn't concern her. That's why her pictures are so full of the unique substance of reality.'[55] *Iskusstvo kino* gave the film respectful treatment, publishing two lead reviews by Plakhov and Igor Mantsov in its August 1994 issue, along with an interview with Litvinova.[56]

Muratova emphatically defended herself from the critical cliché that she had stopped loving people. 'I don't understand what it means to love people. I'm not a cat or the Lord God. I'm a person myself. In order to love people in general, you have to be above them or next to them, or below. I love some people, others, not.' After the Berlin screening, she recalled, a pair of Russians, probably émigrés, yelled at her, 'You hate people! You show crazy people, and you yourself are crazy!' Muratova was grateful for the protective shoulder of Armen Medvedev, then chairman of Goskino, who stepped between her and the enraged couple.[57] It was a profoundly ironic moment, given Muratova's problems with Goskino in its previous Soviet incarnation.

# 6. Crimes Without Punishment: *Three Stories* [1997]

No, you mustn't! Mustn't! Mustn't!

Lilia Murlykina – *Three Stories*

In the first post-Soviet decade Russian directors larded their films with sex and violence in a vain attempt to win back their domestic audience from Hollywood thrillers and action movies. Muratova had long wanted to explore the genre in her own way and for her own purposes. 'After I had made plotless films for a long time – and the majority of my films are without plot, I was then interested in stream of consciousness – I wanted to make a tightly plotted film.' She asked all her 'writing friends' to write screenplays or stories that would be 'simply the story of a crime. Not its consequences, but the crime itself.'[1] Unsure whether she had enough funding to complete a feature-length film and doubting that one plot would provide her enough material, she decided to make three short films, linked by the common theme of murder, as money became available.[2] Her motivation was artistic as well as financial: 'In recent years, it more and more often seems to me that directors of "major films" are artificially stringing out their length, resorting to wordiness without any justification... Or perhaps I love the short film simply because of my own impatience.'[3] *Three Stories* became Muratova's most successful film since *Asthenic Syndrome*. It was also the most controversial.

While her Russian colleagues were competing with Hollywood's second-raters, *Three Stories* took on Quentin Tarantino's *Pulp Fiction* [1994]. Irina Rubanova has noted the similarity in 'characters who are both participants in the plot... plus carriers of a slightly out of synch, but fixed conception of a similar hero, not yet a mask but a clear approximation of one'.[4] Muratova aestheticised the violence to remind the audience this was cinema, not reality, creating a constant counterpoint between the film's beauty and its characters' inhumanity. She gives us four cold-blooded murders: a throat slitting, a strangulation, a drowning and a poisoning; the crimes are carried out, in three cases, right before the eyes of the audience. With marked disdain for Hollywood norms, no firearms are used and relatively little blood is in evidence. These, however, are crimes without punishment – there is no indication that the murderers will be apprehended. Muratova reserves moral judgement, telling her stories with irony and sophistication in the mode of black comedy. James Meek has characterised the film as 'a trio of narratives about women and death [that] combines the surreal, mannered, but precisely aimed plotting of Peter Greenaway with the subtly stylized speech and acting of Sergei Paradjanov, and the virtuoso, painterly use of light and colour of both men'.[5] The film's unpunished crimes may be in some sense the revenge of a film-maker who, throughout her career, was censored and censured for far less grievous offences.

American-style pulp fiction, the grist for Tarantino's ironic mill, was never allowed in tightly controlled Soviet culture, though it has become wildly popular in post-Soviet Russia. The titles of the film's three sections are, instead, tongue-in-cheek references to European high-culture classics: 'Boiler Room No. 6' refers to Chekhov's story 'Ward No. 6', in which a doctor takes to visiting the mental ward for long philosophical conversations with the patients; 'Ophelia' is, of course, Shakespeare's drowned heroine; and 'The Little Girl and Death' echoes the title of Schubert's 14th String Quartet 'Death and the Maiden'.[6] These ironic titles signal Muratova's challenge to the didactic traditions of Russian literature and cinema. But many Russian film critics, still expecting a humanist message from the creator of *Brief Encounters*, *The Long Farewell*, and *Asthenic Syndrome*, were bewildered by Muratova's intentionally distanced authorial stance. 'Muratova no longer loves humanity!' again lamented Turovsky, titling his review 'All people are monsters,'[7] *Itogi*'s reviewer complained that 'Muratova doesn't let us catch her attitude to her own characters – are they monsters or ordinary typical people? Is she passing judgement on man and mankind, or just, in her own way, joking, perhaps?'[8]

In 'Boiler Room No. 6' (screenplay by Igor Bozhko) the sombre Tikhomirov (Sergei Makovetsky) rolls a wardrobe containing the body of a beautiful neighbour from his communal apartment into the boiler room manned by his school friend Gena (Leonid Kushnir). He was forced to kill her, he explains, because she would walk around the apartment nude and give him no peace. He begs Gena to cremate her. Muratova drops plenty of hints, as well as the Chekhovian title, that her parodied subtext is the Russian literary tradition, rich in dead female bodies that return to haunt their murderers: the elderly countess who literally dies of fright in Pushkin's 'The Queen of Spades' and the old pawnbroker in Dostoevsky's *Crime and Punishment*, to name only two.

The title character of Daniil Kharms's absurdist story 'The Old Woman' enters the narrator's apartment without explanation and dies there. His frantic attempt to dispose of the body – by stuffing it in a suitcase and heading for the country on a suburban train – anticipates Tikhomirov's predicament.[9] While Gena makes tea, Tikhomirov begins to philosophise: 'Others go about their life, but I feel like a superfluous man. Do you remember we studied them in school – Pechorin, Onegin?' Makovetsky, one of Russia's best-known film actors, is renowned for his depiction of the Russian 'intelligent', and his costume – homburg, scarf, overcoat – and speech imply that here he is playing to type. Tikhomirov's name is derived from the Russian words for 'quiet' and 'peace'. In mid-1990s Russia, when intellectuals were unemployed and cold-blooded Mafia killings were commonplace, he is both a 'superfluous man', like Pushkin's Eugene Onegin, and an ironic 'hero of our time', like Lermontov's Pechorin.

Gena, in turn, caricatures the generation of the 1970s, when non-conformist artists and intellectuals took jobs as furnace stokers in city apartment houses to ensure themselves living space and ample free time. His perfectly awful verse parodies Russian futurist poetry. To Tikhomirov's complaints about his neighbour, he helpfully suggests, 'Just take an axe and split her head open' (shades of *Crime and Punishment*!), then advises, 'Better you should slit her throat.'[10] 'I sort of did that,' mumbles Tikhomirov, opening the wardrobe to reveal her nude body with a bloody gash across the throat. Though some critics were horrified by this shot, another pointed out that the pool of blood in the hollow of the actress's throat rises and falls with her breathing – Muratova keeps reminding the audience that this is art, not reality. And, by exaggerating the gore, she signals – as Tarantino does – that the appropriate audience reaction is laughter, not horror.

A rotund, pony-tailed, semi-nude homosexual (Jean Daniel) emerges from a door in the corner of Gena's boiler room. 'Veniamin Andreevich,' he intro-duces himself formally, 'but to my friends, simply Venichka' – the well-known nickname of the late Venedikt Erofeev, who chronicled the adventures of a Moscow alcoholic in his novel *Moscow Circles*.[11] Venichka owes Gena money, which he earns by dispensing sexual favours in the shower room. The gloomy boiler room, with its blazing furnace, plays on traditional images of purgatory. But it provides Muratova and Kariuk with opportunities for striking cine-matography – they find beauty in this most unlikely of settings, playing with both natural and artificial light on the pipes, mirrors and dingy walls. And, of course, there is the unsettling beauty of the naked body itself. The novella ends without resolution, as Tikhomirov and Gena sit weeping on the wardrobe, still without a solution to their predicament.

'Ophelia', by far the longest of the three novellas, was based on a scenario by Litvinova, who played the title role.[12] It returns to *The Sentimental Policeman*'s theme of maternal abandonment, but in a very different key: Elena Plakhova has called it 'Secrets and Lies in the Russian manner'.[13] Ophelia/Ofa murders two women in cold blood: Tania (Natalia Buzko), who has just given up her newborn in the maternity home, and Alexandra Ivanovna (Svenskaia), Ofa's own mother, who similarly abandoned her. Ofa is the epitome of sterile beauty, like a marble statue in her physical perfection, but, continuing Muratova's investigation, with no love for anyone: 'I don't love men, I don't love women, I don't love children. I don't like people. I'd give this planet a zero,' she announces to her still-nude partner after a sexual encounter. Her only passion is for the secrets contained in the maternity home's archives.

'Ophelia' is beautiful to watch, like Litvinova herself, on whom the camera lingers long and often. But, says Anna Bossart, 'It is a mistake to regard Litvinova as a femme fatale, for that she is too stylized. Ofa is fate itself.'[14] Her heavily powdered face, critics have noted, gives her the complexion of death. Her cold beauty and cold-blooded revenge set the stylistic and chromatic keys for the section's pre-Christian cultural referents: Greek, Roman and Old Testament. The moral criterion here is not guilt but fate, the subject of a long monologue by Ofa herself. Her pale complexion, platinum hair, white uniform, cream-coloured coat and red nails, lipstick, dress, gloves and purse set the novella's chromatic key of white and red. In the opening shot, a stream of doctors and nurses in white uniforms descends the white neoclassical stairway of the maternity home. Litvinova ascends against the human stream, pausing to tie on a gauze mask with the now familiar mannered movements of her red-tipped fingers. Her movements are markedly snake-like and her voice hypnotic as she parks herself on Tania's pillow; several golden apples are visible on the bedside table. The Edenic reference is clear, but Ofa is there not to tempt Tania, rather to warn against making the wrong choice: 'I'm still your friend, and don't turn me into the opposite.'

Ivan Okhlobystin, like Litvinova a fashionable Moscow celebrity of the mid-1990s (he is an actor, film director, television personality and screenwriter), plays a gynaecologist in dogged pursuit of Ofa. They smoke and banter in front of three backgrounds covering the gamut of the spiritual and the material: a representation of the Sistine Madonna etched on glass, a display case of instruments for birthing and abortion, and an anatomy chart of the human brain. As always in Muratova, the *mise en scène* is as important as the action taking place within it, and there is usually an ironic play between them. After work, he strolls with Ofa through a graffiti-covered neoclassical colonnade by the Odessa waterfront, once used by Eisenstein for a striking shot in *Battleship Potemkin*.[15] Ofa hastily cancels their assignation when he mentions that Tania has given up her child and discharged herself from the hospital. She rushes back in time to see Tania, clicking her heels along the corridor, stroll smugly out of the maternity home, as a child's cry is heard on the soundtrack.

Ofa follows Tania across a weed-covered hillside and a construction site, where Tania squats and urinates. Ofa, framed in a doorway behind her, does the same. This public female urination, and the twinned episode of male urination that closely follows it, are as much of a 'slap in the face of public taste' as the homosexual prostitution in the first episode. But Muratova presents both in a matter-of-fact manner, like the episode of obscene language at the end of *Asthenic Syndrome*. Her intent may be similar, for in the courtyards of Russian city buildings the scent of urine follows one almost like the foul language that Muratova has described as 'ubiquitous as birdsong'. As Ofa lures her quarry into an entryway, Tania fulminates at a man urinating in the courtyard: 'Cretin! I hate men!' Ofa agrees: 'I hate men. I hate women.' 'Whom, then, do you like?' inquires Tania, in what will be her last words. 'I love children. Turn away,' commands Ofa, and, calmly removing her stocking, uses it to strangle Tania from behind. Straddling the body, she experiences an orgasm.

She then phones the doctor to resume their assignation, perhaps to establish an alibi. Two non-diegetic shots of an Ionic column bracket their sexual encounter. A female index finger, presumably Ofa's, with its bright red nail, traces the indented spiral pattern on the capitol four times. There is something erotic about this sequence and its twin, though it is difficult to say what. The double spiral pattern suggests graphically simplified fallopian tubes and ovaries, uniting the maternity that Ofa and her mother both reject with the architecture of archaic Greece. The assignation takes place in the studio of the doctor's artist friend. Muratova's camera leisurely scans the pictures on the walls (they are actually conceptualist paintings by Golubenko). We witness only the aftermath of the sexual encounter, with the sleeping doctor, nude except for his socks, sprawled on the sofa. Nonchalantly, Ofa extracts herself from his embrace and returns to the scene of the crime, where she has forgotten her purse under Tania's body.[16] It lies undisturbed, guarded only by a kindly hound dog (a wickedly delightful Muratova touch). I. Gladilshchikov has commented that, in this film, nude male bodies are repulsive (he cites the pudgy Venichka as well as the unromantic doctor) while nude female bodies are aestheticised (Tikhomirov's neighbour in 'Boiler Room No. 6' and the child in 'The Little Girl and Death' as well as Ofa herself). 'The absence of normal men in Muratova's films isn't new,' he comments. '"Man" with a capital "M" has died.'[17]

Ophelia, entrusted for the first time with the keys to the archive, unearths her mother's address.[18] Alexandra Ivanovna shares Ofa's platinum blonde hair and bright red lipstick, though she is as portly as Ofa is svelte. Alexandra refuses to open the door to a stranger, but, when she looks out, Ofa – her back to the window – symbolically uses her own pocket mirror to study her mother's face. Alexandra emerges in the morning wearing a capacious red dress in exactly the same shade and style as Ofa's, though many sizes larger. Natalia Svirilia observes that the novella is constructed on doubles: 'two murders, two abandoned children…the repeated dialogue, gestures, and the "refined and malicious" rhyming of Ofa with Alexandra.'[19] As Ofa follows her downhill to the harbour[20] they pass an elderly woman on the street, who

13. *Three Stories*: Natalia Buzko, Renata Litvinova

calls 'Mama!' to a still more ancient lady on a balcony. 'I'm so worried about you!' 'Why don't you call?' cries the deaf mother. 'I'm very worried, why don't you pick up the phone?' the daughter replies; the exchange is repeated several times. The bitter-sweet comic vignette, which comments on the mutual isolation of Ofa and her mother, seems different in style and tone from the rest of this novella. In fact, it was inserted into Litvinova's screenplay by Muratova, who originally conceived the episode as a class project while still at VGIK.

Alexandra Ivanovna sits on a wharf reading a book about her favourite heroine – Ophelia, of course. Ofa insinuates herself next to her mother, pesters her like a toddler seeking attention. She rests her head on her mother's shoulder, evoking only an eye roll of amazement. Ofa drops broad hints about being an orphan, but Alexandra ignores them. So Ofa throws the book into the water and shoves her mother in after it. Taking a cigarette lighter, she sets fire to her mother's file, holds it as it burns, then shudders with another orgasm. Leaving the wharf, she hands Alexandra's cane, her only inheritance from her mother, to two blind men. Alexander Rutkovsky comments, 'Having given one "code", Hamlet, Muratova shifted in the finale to Lear – "In our age the mad lead the blind."'[21]

In 'The Little Girl and Death', a small girl poisons the elderly, wheel-chair-bound neighbour who watches her while her mother works. The novella opens with an hilariously macabre sequence in which a howling black cat torments the carcass of a plucked chicken. The episode has been read either as a sign that Muratova has lost even her faith in animals or that the bestiality displayed by her murderers is inherent in humanity. 'The Little Girl and Death' is a duel between the nameless old man (Oleg Tabakov) and the five-year-old Lilia Murlykina (her real name). Her first name, Lilia, echoes that of Litvinova's character in *Enthusiasms*, while her family name, derived from the Russian word 'to purr', perhaps explains the abundance of cats in the novella. Lilia wants to play with his coffee grinder, to go out in the street. To all her requests, he answers, 'You mustn't!' (*nel'zia*), trying instead to impart moral maxims and chess lessons. Theirs is a clash not only of generations but of social class. Tabakov's Moscow Art Theatre diction, his chessboard, the fan inherited from his grandmother, the old romances he hums under his breath, all identify him as a member of the old intelligentsia. Lilia's mother works in a cafeteria, and the girl's speech parrots her working-class intonations and resentments. 'I'm not going to stay with you. You can't walk. No one will bring you groceries. When you die we'll pri-va-tise your apartment.' The old man counters with a threat to denounce her mother for 'privatising' *pirozhki* from the cafeteria. The argument escalates until the girl leaves the terrace and collects mouse traps (complete with dangling dead mice) from around the apartment. She mixes the remaining rat poison with water and brings it to the old man in a white enamel cup, which masks its milky colour. As the poison goes to work, the old man phones an anonymous friend and begins a lengthy monologue on old age. 'Do you understand, you can love an old man or old woman only if you really, really love them. I mean, you can, with difficulty, tolerate them, pity them, forgive them – yes, forgive – them for their old age. Old age is regarded as a crime. People want to punish you, humiliate you, liquidate you, send you to the devil and get you out of their sight.' In mid-sentence, he sighs deeply and gives up the ghost. Lilia triumphantly runs off the terrace to freedom, skipping among golden apples and mocking his repeated 'No, you mustn't!' Indeed she can – and she does. Maya Turovskaya has noted that the insouciant Lilia, not accidentally, looks very much the way Muratova herself would have looked as a child.[22]

Muratova's cold-blooded child-murderess has particularly troubled many critics, and the film's 'retreat from humanism' stirred up a huge critical debate.[23] Having the little Lilia Murlykina play a character with her own name was beyond the pale, some felt, as it implied that any normal girl can kill. Arkhangelsky points to the choice of Tabakov, and the scene of the two deaf old ladies in 'Ophelia', as signs that '[Muratova] wanted in advance to be mistaken in her verdict [about humanity], and chose a lawyer who could weaken the pathos of her accusation'.[24] Anna Koroleva thinks that Muratova intended this last novella as an answer to the first, in which she would resurrect 'the vitality murdered by Makovetsky's hero'. Little Lilia (who also walks about naked at one point) would take revenge on the tedious old man, the double of Tikhomirov's 'intelligent' in the film's first episode. 'But the director was undone by the brilliant Oleg Tabakov, who played with a jewelled precision of each word, but with the absolute, classical directness of a true son of Stanislavsky.'[25] In Vera Storozheva's original screenplay the babysitter was an old woman, so Tabakov was startled when Muratova phoned to offer him the role. 'I began to explain to Kira that I would never take on old women's roles in the cinema…to which Kira replied, "Don't worry, Oleg. I'll rewrite the whole thing." And really, she turned it into a masculine role, adding a marvellous monologue…about old age, uselessness, being a burden for those around one.' Tabakov called the role 'Perhaps, despite its small size, one of my favourites on the screen'.[26]

In addition to its rich subtexts from antiquity and Russian literature, *Three Stories* is full of ironic self-quotations and familiar faces from Muratova's own work. There are two more plastic dolls and return appearances by several favourite actors. But most obvious is the comparison of animals and people. The film opens in a zoo, where Tikhomirov stares at an elephant with a broken tusk and imitates a peacock. Ofa reads Zola's *Animals and People*. There is the dog guarding Tania's body and the unforgettable cats in 'The Little Girl and Death'.

While Muratova had always drawn superlative performances from relatively unknown actors, in *Three Stories* she instead used two established super-stars, Makovetsky and Tabakov, along with Litvinova, the new star she had created herself. But she still preferred to mix them with 'eccentric' actors and non-professionals:

> Makovetsky was filmed with Kushnir. Makovetsky in his pure form would not have suited me. This combination of non-professional and actor works very well for me. Like Tabakov and the little girl... Kushnir with his incorrect pronunciation, his crazy rhetorical intonations somehow bothers Makovetsky, he's irritated that Kushnir is like that... While at the same time there emerges, even just a little bit, something rough and unprofessional in Makovetsky.

14. *Three Stories*: Renata Litvinova, Alexandra Svenskaia

Muratova was quite taken with little Murlykina: 'She's very talented. It's not just that she knows how to act, but the girl very quickly sensed the pleasure in acting, and that's the main thing you can get from a non-professional.' Of Okhlobystin paired with Litvinova she observed:

> He's a very good actor, but he's not spontaneous, on the contrary, he's very consciously decisive. Renata – not at all. Because she's a very strong personality, and this doesn't allow for a precise expression in words, there's an impulsiveness in her...She's not afraid of herself...She behaves freely and wilfully because of her beauty, precisely her beauty, because she knows that she'll always be liked.[27]

The working title of the film was 'Sad Stories' [Grustnye istorii], but Muratova found that too sentimental. Filming was to have been finished by the spring of 1996, but funding ran out in December 1995, after only 'Boiler Room No. 6' had been shot. Shooting of the last two novellas resumed in Odessa in the autumn of 1996. *Three Stories* premiered in mid-February 1997 at the Berliniale, one of twenty-five films in competition with *The English Patient*. There was hope that it might win Muratova another Silver Bear, but when it did not her defenders suggested that the jury was looking for another *Asthenic Syndrome*. *Three Stories* also failed to win a prize at the annual Kinotavr Festival of Russian films at Sochi.

In slight violation of the Berliniale's rules, the Moscow premiere took place in the jam-packed hall of Dom Kino on the eve of the festival's opening. Bossart defended the film: 'Perhaps Muratova is brutal, but not cold. Her passion is the measured flame of a scholar in search of truth. We wouldn't ask a microbiologist seeking a vaccine against AIDS to love his mice...Kira Muratova has a striking sense of humour and knows, perhaps better than anyone else, how to use it in the cinema.'[28] Arkhangelsky pointed to the film's myriad internal connections and echoes: 'Muratova's apotheosis of the aimlessness of existence is constructed with rare purposefulness; a film about the utmost disharmony is organized with marvellous harmony.' But he, like many reviewers, wrestled with the question of Muratova's authorial stance. 'Incompatible with both the "laughter through tears" inherited by the Russian tradition from Gogol, and the tubercular mockery of the late Chekhov, who has lost all hope but preserved at least nostalgia for lost faith,... her smile in *Three Stories* is rather the icy smile of indifference...not from callousness, but from the consciousness of doom.' He feared that, if she continued in this vein, she would end in silence, like the 'genius of evil' Vladimir Sorokin, or like Petrushevskaia, who, he claimed, had 'forgotten how to write' after *The Time: Night*.[29] The St Petersburg film journal *Seans* published two reviews and selection of opinions from fifteen more critics. Turovskaya: 'Brilliant directing. The contents aren't meant to be taken seriously. This is pure form, like a horror film. The television screen shows us more horrific things.' Plakhov: 'It's pleasant that the demands for humanism in film art have again been renewed – precisely in connection with Muratova.' Svirilia: 'The film mercilessly destroys the postmodernist illusion that a world can survive in which everything that makes man "the image of his maker" has lost its meaning – love, culture, morality.'[30]

In September 1997, responding to the 'stormy discussions of the film that have continued for half a year', *Iskusstvo kino* published six more views by a wide range of film critics and historians. Rubanova:

> Muratova always has the miraculous ability the turn the usually uncinematic – in the sense of narration, or type of performance – into the irresistibly cinematic... Her humour... with all its strangeness, has no equals in our cinema or beyond... In *Three Stories*, evidently Muratova planned to unite both these talents – to show the terrible as funny.

But paradoxically, she has made 'perhaps her most social picture'.[31] Viktor Erofeev: 'Muratova is perhaps the only one in our cinema who has responded to the general turning point in art at the end of the twentieth century away from the investigation of external evil to the study of internal evil.'[32] Nina Tsirkun:

> *Three Stories*... is a light-hearted film, otherwise, I think, the author wouldn't have dedicated it to her teacher Sergei Gerasimov, lover of men and their souls... If you reverse the first and last episodes, you can read it as the story of one woman... then it becomes the story of crime and punishment, and a place is found for humanist pathos.

'The Little Girl and Death' did, in fact, originally come first, but Muratova changed the final order of the three novellas. Tsirkun characterised them as, in that order, 'an eccentric comedy, a parody of a thriller, and a parody of Lolita/Barbie'.[33]

Oleg Aronson analysed the film in terms of three key concepts of the Russian avant-garde: formalist literary theorist Viktor Shklovsky's concepts of the device and of defamiliarisation, and Sergei Eisenstein's concept of the cinematographic attraction. Aronson argues that Muratova is a formalist, and we can readily agree. But Shklovsky's concept of defamiliarisation is linguistically based – it aims at making us 'see things anew, without their usual names and associations'. Cinema, however, already sees things. Muratova, therefore,

> strives for an artistic representation that will be so direct that what is seen on the screen will appear strange because we refuse to look at it in life, but in the movie theatre we are forced to look... Muratova's task is not to seek out shocking material, but to take it from ordinary life, where we have got so accustomed to it that we perceive it automatically... or to single out those moments when we automatically, reflexively, turn off our vision... This is not yet a device, but already an attraction.

Aronson takes the term from Eisenstein's 'Montage of Attractions' – 'a deliberate and constructed element of affective influence on the viewer' – which, he explains, serves in the visual medium of film the function served by the literary device of defamiliarisation: to make us see things anew. Her mechanical repetition of speech, he argues, 'forces us not to hear the words, intonations, faces, objects, but precisely to "read" them. She continually "distances" her subject in order to capture the world in the mechanism of our perception.'[34] Aronson's analysis reminds us yet again how often the finger-prints of the avant-garde appear in Muratova's films. And it helps us make artistic sense of those elements in her film-making that offend critics rooted in a traditional Russian didactic mode of reading.

She planned a sequel to *Three Stories* starring Litvinova and using two more scenarios proposed for the original film. According to Muratova, the stories were barely connected, but they were to alternate 'two women, two killers; one was rather kind, the other evil: evil Faina, kind Klavdia'. Litvinova offered to find a producer for their project. She approached Alexander Antipov, and, according to Muratova, 'she found him as a producer, and in the process of these searches and conversations she fell in love with him and married him'. Then, she recalled, he raised objections to Muratova's changes in Litvinova's screenplay:

> I always add some bits to the shooting script. I'm one person, Renata is another, although I'm crazy about what she writes. Renata's story was possible for me as one of three stories, but as an entire film it wasn't enough for me, I begin to gasp for breath, I need a spoonful of tar [a Russian proverb meaning 'fly in the ointment']. I begin to stick some old grannies into the film. She likes that, but at the same time she senses something…She likes it as art, but at the same time she wants to be the prima donna in the shot, a diva, to reign all the time. And I also want her to reign, but it seems to me that she will be even more majestic in contrast if you put some kind of freak next to her.

Antipov sent faxes demanding specific cuts. When he asked for her reaction, she replied, 'I feel such nostalgia, I thought Pavlenok [the notoriously con-servative head of the old Soviet Goskino] had written to me.' He retorted, 'Well, perhaps Pavlenok was right about some things.' When he continued his categorical demands, 'in Hollywood fashion,' she told him, 'Well, you can go to hell. Film it yourself. I don't want to.'[35] Fiercely independent, even at the risk of sacrificing a film project, Muratova resisted compromise, just as she had in the years under Pavlenok's Goskino.

# 7. Muratova as a Ukrainian Film-maker

After the break-up of the USSR in 1991 Muratova became even more of an outsider – a Romanian-born Russian-speaking citizen of independent Ukraine who continued to make her films in Russian in the multilingual, multi-ethnic 'city state' of Odessa. Much of her funding, audience and critical attention at first continued to come from Russian sources. The Odessa Studio, along with the rest of the Ukrainian film industry, fell on hard times. But, since Muratova was almost the only active film-maker in Ukraine with an international reputation, the Ukrainian press began paying more attention to her work. *Three Stories* won the first Arsenal award as the best Ukrainian film of 1997, and in 1999 Muratova was given a $50,000 award by the Centre for the Development of Ukrainian Cinema.[1] *Minor People* [2001] and *Chekhov's Motifs* [2002] were funded largely with support from the Ukrainian Ministry of Culture, whose vice-minister, Hanna Chmiel, served as the films' co-producer, along with the Odessa local and regional administrations. Though the financial resources Ukraine could provide were relatively modest, never before in her career had Muratova been able to shoot two films in successive years.

In several ways these late films move onto new ground, and in others they return to the aesthetic of her early films, but in a new tonality. To economise on costly film stock, she used a minimal number of takes, adding to the sense of improvisation. The films feature Odessa actors in distinctively local settings. Though Odessa's distinctive south Russian accent was often heard in Muratova's earlier work in the speech of her non-professionals, she now exaggerated it in the speech of almost all her actors. But, despite the provincial settings, Muratova remained emphatically universal in her themes. Her latest films have textual and thematic links to three great masters of Russian prose fiction – Dostoevsky, Gogol and Chekhov.

## *Letter to America* [1999]

Two years after the *succès de scandale* of *Three Stories* Muratova was still struggling to find funding for a screenplay the provisional title of which, 'Reverses of Fortune', ironically echoed *A Change of Fate*. After the Russian financial crash of 1998 funding was hard enough to come by for Moscow film-makers, but for Muratova the search was particularly difficult. She was remote from the wealthy New Russians in Moscow, and, moreover, not particularly good at fund-raising. 'Those who know how to do it, get money, and that's a wonderful quality. That's just not my sport... When I try to raise money, I lose my taste for the future film and I need some time to fall into depression and then pull myself out of it.'[2] Her 'depression' could be cured only by what she termed her favourite 'narcotic' – shooting a film. This was the primary motivation for *Letter to America*,[3] a twenty-minute two-reeler. The film was made with little or no money; all four actors live in Odessa and worked for free. Poet Sergei Chetverkov wrote the screenplay and played Oleg; Ute Kilter, an art critic, played Lena. Both had played cameo roles in previous Muratova films. Nikolai Sednev (the nameless cameraman) was a director at the Odessa studio; Pavel Makarov (Lena's lover) his assistant. The film was shot in two days in Muratova's own apartment and in a park nearby. Even Lena's dress, borrowed for the occasion, is credited. Originally, she planned to shoot on video, but Kodak film stock was found.

*Letter to America* is a black comedy about the desperate predicament of post-Soviet intellectuals, similar in that sense to Kiev film-maker Viacheslav Krishtofovich's *A Friend of the Deceased* ['Priiatel' pokoinika', 1997]. Oleg, an unemployed poet, sits overlooking the Odessa port recounting an empty life: 'I haven't married, I'm not working... I feel OK, I still like to drink, you see I've started smoking again.' The cameraman is shooting a video to send to Oleg's former girlfriend in America. Prompted to say more, Oleg produces a string of incongruously meaningless Soviet-era clichés: '*No passeran!* If not we, then who else! We can't retreat – Moscow is behind us!' These catch-phrases were used by the Soviet elite, 'which believed that precisely they were responsible for everything. For ethics and morality, particularly,' notes Elena Stishova. In the post-Soviet era Muratova could openly parody such empty slogans, and the attitudes that underlay them. Stishova argues that 'Muratova, for all her aesthetic radicalism, never breaks with reality... *Letter to America* is a comedy of manners filmed like a documentary, with irony, sarcasm, and an openly publicistic message.'[4]

To support himself, Oleg has rented out his apartment to Lena, a woman of unspecified profession, and bunks with friends. But she is two months behind on the rent. Hostage to his intelligentsia values, Oleg finds it difficult to demand his money. Lena claims to be penniless, but offers to pay 'in kind'. He declines; it is a luxury he can't afford. Gathering his resolve, he returns to find her with a half-naked young man, who has emerged from the wardrobe – the classic trope of bedroom farce. Commanding Oleg to wait in the kitchen, Lena counts out some money from her hidden reserves, then emerges with partial payment. Evoking *Crime and Punishment*'s Sonia Marmeladova, she implies she has sold her body to the young man, 'a co-worker who happened to drop by – better than a total stranger'. She adds, with pseudo-Dostoevskian pathos, 'I borrowed two rubles because I'm out of bread.' In case we miss the subtexts, she mutters while watering Oleg's plants: 'Fyodor Mikhailovich Dostoevsky hiccups, rejoices and turns over in his grave.'

Muratova described the film as provincial, the characters as Chekhovian: 'It has a lot of local colour. This is not a Moscow tale – here your intellectuals are more active and try to do something, but in Odessa they sit, write letters somewhere, hate, complain, complain some more, without undertaking anything. Like Chekhov's characters. They write wonderful poetry, but they have no energy for anything else.'[5] Oleg and his friend the cameraman are modern underground men who take a perverse pride in their poverty, sloth, deception and humiliation, defiantly resentful of friends who have emigrated to America only to send back the occasional gift of cheap clothing. Meeting in the park to finish the video, they recite into the camera Oleg's 'Ode to an Émigré'.

> Where were you, where were you, when we sat here
> and, elbowing each other round the table,
> ate for hours, then drank for hours,
> endlessly annoying the neighborhood?

The cameraman spits defiantly into the lens, then, with no sense of incongruity, enquires whether Oleg's raincoat is a present from America. The two walk off, embracing, in a parody of American buddy films, as the soundtrack plays an aria from, appropriately, *La Bohème*.[6]

Muratova's film is *itself* a letter to America. One of its not so hidden messages is an ironic self-commentary on Muratova's own situation, an example of what talent can do even in poverty, and a protest against the increasing dependence on expensive special effects that forced Russian film-makers to 'prostitute' their art. In 1999 over $20 million from the Russian state budget went to finance Nikita Mikhalkov's $45 million *Barber of Siberia* in a futile quest to win an Oscar. At the press conference following the premiere of *Letter to America*, Muratova was in a sprightly mood. Someone asked: 'Kira Georgievna, if they gave you $45 million and proposed that you film a blockbuster, would you agree?' Muratova replied,

> I don't need that much money. You know…I was taught from the very beginning that you've got to tell the administrators: 'But I shoot cheap films! What would it

cost you to give me just a little bit of money, even if I film ideologically incorrectly?' And, imagine, under the influence of those words you gradually begin to form an aesthetic of the type 'humility is better than pride'. You may need 45 million bucks, but I don't. I need just a little bit, and I'll do it marvellously.[7]

There is yet another, more coded, message in *Letter to America*.[8] The words of Oleg's poem are difficult to make out, since he and the cameraman recite it not quite in unison. But the poem, referred to as 'an epistle to a traveller, or to a pilgrim', is in fact addressed to the late Nobel Laureate Joseph Brodsky. The first lines give us a clue:

> The donkey cries, the cow lows, they have wakened the Christ child.
> And he is silent?

Brodsky was known for his yearly Christmas poems with their frequent evocations of the manger scene.[9] In the Russian text of Oleg's ode we hear Brodsky's lexicon and frequently used anapestic meter:

> To this day we recall your missive
> With its receptions, conversations, landscapes,
> A myriad of place names, a verse in Latin...

The poem ends with bitter defiance, the verbal equivalent of spittle directed at the camera lens:

> May you be damned! And damn your walking staff,
> Your groves, lakes, and hills.
> Don't disturb our fortress-like boredom
> Don't write! And if you return, we'll strangle you
> With the strap of your traveling bag.

The poem, perhaps an improvisation, is not in the original screenplay, which ended simply with a question directed at the camera: 'Do you over there ever feel like throwing up?'

Muratova finished *Letter to America* just in time for the 21st Moscow International Film Festival in June 1999. It was screened in Venice at the Mostra International Festival in September. In October it had its Ukrainian premiere at the Kiev Film Actors' Festival 'Stozhary', and at the Kiev International Film Festival 'Molodist' (Youth) it was voted 'Best Ukrainian Film of 1999'. Thanks to the German film scholar Hans Joachim Schlegel, it was included in the 2000 Berliniale, at which Muratova was awarded the $50,000 Andrzej Wajda Freedom Prize, sponsored by Phillip Morris. Muratova announced she would use the award to begin shooting her next feature film.

## *Minor People* [2001]

Muratova described *Minor People* as 'a rather modest film, tranquil and pacifying',[10] and labelled it 'a moderate thriller with elements of vaudeville'. The title, which, literally, means 'second-class people', recalls both 'superfluous people' (*lishnye liudi*), a hallowed concept in traditional histories of Russian literature, and *Poor Folk* [Bednye liudi], the title of Dostoevsky's early sentimental novel in letters.[11] *Minor People* continues the black humour of *Letter to America* and *Three Stories*, though it treats death in a more eccentric way, and with a 'happy end'. It begins with a death imminently anticipated, moves to a death totally unexpected, then on to a Mafia-style execution forestalled by the victim's sudden death in the trunk of a car, ending with the equally unexpected return to life of the corpse that the central character has been trying, through much of the film, to dispose of.

The action and acting are absurdist. A district doctor (Chetverkov, who also wrote the screenplay) visits a dying patient in a wealthy family of 'New Ukrainians'. An icon surrounded by blinking Christmas lights defines their 'spirituality'. The house is part of an unfinished settlement of oversized brick 'cottages' built by the post-Soviet nouveau riche. We hear the squeal of a pig and the cries of people chasing it. Two women on cheek-by-jowl balconies verbally abuse each other in a sequence that recalls the street scene in *The Sentimental Policeman*: 'Perhaps they're killing someone.' 'I couldn't care less [*mne naplevat*'].' 'I couldn't care less that you couldn't care less.' Finally, we see the pig chase, magnificently photographed against the behemoths of half-built villas. The pig rooting in a mud puddle evokes the early stories of Gogol, like Muratova a Russian/Ukrainian master of the absurd. Reviewer Dmitri Bykov singles out the episode for its 'almost Bruegel-like power',[12] and Muratova has confided that it is her favourite sequence in the film.[13]

Vera (Buzko) asks the doctor for help in subduing a drunken companion, Vasia (Sednev), who is threatening to burn down the house. As Vasia is about to hit the doctor over the head with a gasoline canister he falls on his back, motionless, and the doctor, after a quick examination, declares in alarm: 'I think he's dead.' Vera intentionally ignores his frantic cries to call an ambulance. They stuff the body into a large rolling suitcase. The next day, Vera sets off to dispose of the suitcase. When she stops by the post office where she works, opposite the madhouse, the costumed madmen form another Bruegel-like procession in the background. Misha (Filip Panov), a young resident of the madhouse, offers to help her with the suitcase. She encounters more strange types on her odyssey, including an exhibitionist. Vera and Misha store the suitcase with left luggage at Odessa's cruise ship port, populated for the occasion by singing and dancing eccentrics no less odd than the denizens of the madhouse.[14] Misha refuses to hand over the chit, which he is saving for his album of curiosities. Vera is saved by an unexpected reversal of fate – Vasia inexplicably emerges from the suitcase alive and well.

The film has a second storyline; in fact, the script was based on two different novellas by Chetverkov.[15] Vasia, it turns out, is the identical twin of Alexei (Sednev played both twins), who works as a bodyguard for Jean (Jean Daniel), a gangster of self-described 'Caucasian nationality' and the owner of the unfinished house where Vera lives. A female police inspector drops by, looking for information not about Vasia but about a 'dismembered corpse found last week in the courtyard of a house up the street'. If Vera's behaviour has been eccentrically theatrical, Jean's is over the top. He enquires exactly which parts of the body were found, adding gratuitously, 'They say it was a hermaphrodite ... In general, women should not be killed, they should be raped ... so that the human race would continue, although, however, why should it continue, as the great Tolstoy said.' Jean's passing reference to *Kreutzer Sonata* is not surprising; he is a former high school teacher of Russian literature. While the film toys with such high culture referents, including the works in Jean's art collection, scattered throughout the house, its plot situations – palming off a corpse as a drunk, mistaking one twin for the other, narrowly escaping police scrutiny – are classic low culture eccentric comedy. The mixing of cultural codes intensifies the absurdity.

Muratova's send-up of Russian gangster films produces one of the film's funniest sequences. Alexei drives Jean to the shore of the ocean in a vintage white limousine. Jean has taken out a contract on his nemesis, Bul' (Ruslan Khvastov),[16] who once taught physical education in the school where Jean taught Russian literature, but is now also a gangster. The contract, fate would have it, was assigned to Bul' himself. Having taken the down payment, he is obligated to kill himself, but who, he asks in a letter to Jean, will receive the rest of the payment, and who will avenge him, orphan that he is?[17] Alexei refuses to kill a bound man (Bul' is in the trunk of the car) – his job, he says, is bodyguard, not killer. And Jean couldn't possibly do it: 'for ten years I taught children about Raskolnikov's pangs of guilt.' Their moral quandary unexpectedly resolves itself; when they open the trunk, Bul' is dead.

Vera's repetitious speech and exaggerated pronunciation, like Kilter's in *Letter to America*, seem to parody even Muratova's customary estrangement of language. In the shooting script, her unnatural manner is compared to the reading of blank verse. The doubling of her speech underlines the abundance of doubles in the film, another favourite theme of both Gogol (*The Nose*) and Dostoevsky (*The Double*). Sergei Trimbach points out not only that Vasia and Alexei are identical twins but that Bul' is Jean's 'demonic double', who seduced students and the school director while Jean lectured his students about Raskolnikov. Jean's hypertrophic annoyance with Bul' comes from his desire to 'destroy the demonic double'. Jean and Misha, Trimbach observes, are both collectors – Jean of art, or art reproductions (themselves doubles), and Misha of trivial everyday signs of the times, such as theatre posters and Gorbachev buttons.[18] Jean first appears in the film accompanied by a life-size portrait (his 'double'). In an eye-catching sequence, Vera, after Vasia's 'death', stands biting her nails near a large reproduction of Liotard's *Chocolate Girl* (1743–1745), her pose a mirror image of that in the painting. Misha, Trimbach maintains, is the only character 'identical to himself', with no 'other' hidden in him.[19] But he is an 'idiot' in the Dostoevskian mould, a holy fool like Prince Myshkin, and becomes the helpmate of Vera, whose name in Russian means 'faith'.

To some critics and viewers, Muratova seemed to be repeating motifs from earlier films. But Kiev film scholar Oleksii Koniukh objects. 'In reality, this film is much brighter and wiser... Sarcasm has been replaced by bitter irony. And the result is a real comedy, a comedy of our life.' He, like Stishova, argues that Muratova's absurd was the most realistic mode for depicting post-Soviet reality, which she does with an unsettling detachment:

> In Europe, Muratova's films are greatly respected, seen as a sort of surrealism. No one there would imagine that you could actually live this way. In Ukraine, as in Russia, these films are so realistic, they so honestly illuminate the contemporary situation of our existence, that in their strange, often lunatic characters we stubbornly refuse to recognise ourselves and those around us.[20]

Viktoria Belopolskaia argues that Muratova has always been a diagnostician – not a surprising talent for the daughter of a physician.

> When Muratova filmed *Brief Encounters* she was a psychologist. When *The Long Farewell* – a psychoanalyst specialising in 'female neuroses'. In *Asthenic Syndrome* – a psychiatrist (with a special interest in sociopaths)...But now, filming *Minor People*, it's as if our great director has burst into the hysterical laughter characteristic of Dostoevsky's most nervous heroes.[21]

She dubbed the film a 'psychocomedy' and praised its 'gags of truly Chaplin-esque sweep'. Bykov reads the happy ending as a sign of a sea change in Russian cinema after the first post-Soviet decade. Corpses, he observes, were only too evident in Russian films of the period. It is as if 'All this time we have been carrying around, with a great song and dance, the corpse of our former life and former Motherland'.[22]

Muratova, following in the footsteps of Paradjanov, continues to be a visual artist in her films. The prominence she gives to the colourful Armenian Jean Daniel in *Three Stories*, *Minor People* and *Chekhov's Motifs* continues the homage: Daniel was at one time a member of Paradjanov's Tbilisi circle. *Minor People* is filled with beautifully composed frames and sequences, and eye-catching but loosely connected tableaux, such as the pig chase. The film's loose structure is much like Misha's album of photographs, postcards and odd bits of realia, which Muratova uses to present the final credits. By placing them within Misha's album, Muratova identifies herself and her collaborators with its eclecticism and lack of rational structure. Neya Zorkaya was struck by the bright colours of the film, comparing its saturated palette to that of *Getting to Know the Big, Wide World*. 'Yes, in our post-Soviet "sotsiium" these people are marginal, but they're not "ordinary" – rather, original, beautiful, interesting, unpredictable, keen, artistic... like the bright colours of the film.'[23] Muratova

15. *Minor People*: Sergei Chetverkov, Natalia Buzko (photo credit: E. Golubenko)

gave the brunette Buzko major roles in both *Minor People* and *Chekhov's Motifs*, filling the large gap left by her break with the blonde Litvinova. Neither the screenwriter Litvinova nor the mime and comedienne Buzko is an actress in the traditional sense. It was easier for Buzko to adopt the artificial intonation Muratova demanded of her, as it was for Muratova's other new favourite, Panov, a professional model. Each adapted to being made part of the *mise en scène*, to be manipulated by Muratova like a puppet or a doll.

Muratova began preparatory work on the film in 1999 and filmed in the autumn of 2000, finishing just in time for the film's premiere at the Berliniale in February 2001. But, due to the sponsors' haste, it was sent without subtitles. Muratova's German fans sat out fifteen minutes or so but then disappeared, leaving the Russian-speaking contingent of film critics – always Muratova's biggest supporters – laughing uproariously.[24] But the lack of subtitles severely limited the film's exposure to an international critical audience, while its debut in Berlin restricted the number of other festivals in which it could be entered. It won the Grand Prize at the Wiesbaden Festival of Films from Central and Eastern Europe, and was shown at the London Film Festival in November. But it was withdrawn by the Ukrainian authorities from the 2001 New York Festival of New Russian Films because it was a Ukrainian film, not a Russian one. Such absurdities continue to dog Muratova's professional career, and undoubtedly feed the rich vein of black humour in her films.

Muratova made a brief trip to Moscow – she is there far less frequently since Ukrainian independence – for the film's Russian premiere in March 2001 at Dom Khanzhonkova, one of the few Moscow venues devoted to showing Russian-language films. It was in competition at the annual Kinotavr Festival in Sochi in June 2001, but won nothing from a jury that seemed obsessed with encouraging 'popular' Russian cinema. She did win the FIPRESCI film critics' award. The film entered general distribution in Moscow only in May 2002, more than a year after its debut in Berlin. Moscow reviewers generally liked the film. 'Anyone who doesn't see it and judges our "auteur" kino by Sokurov alone will miss a lot. Besides Pechorins [Lermontov's Byronic "hero of our time"], Russian culture is founded on Bashmachkins [the humble hero of Gogol's *The Overcoat*] ... Muratova remains the unchallenged master of the episode.'[25] *Izvestiia* commented on Muratova's 'complete absence of any moralizing. Only in her choice of material is there a very severe, unshakeable system of moral values', making the film 'severe in a masculine way, good-hearted in a feminine way'.[26] *Nezavisimaia gazeta* praised her as 'A director of rare freedom, which annoys many really "second-class" people', and pronounced the film 'the funniest and most unfettered in her oeuvre. Muratova is a Russo-Ukrainian Chaplin – our eccentric and marvellous Aunt Charlie'.[27] '*Minor People* is not for everyone, but for the pleasure of those who are prepared to meet with reality on the screen, garnished with the sauce of the absurd,'[28] added another reviewer.

Some critics were disturbed by the scene of a man French-kissing his beloved monkey, a seeming provocation like the caged dogs and the profanity in *Asthenic Syndrome*, or the child poisoner in *Three Stories*. But Trimbach saw it as another instance in which Muratova uses animals as a moral yardstick for humans: 'Whenever Vera kisses someone, it's because she wants something.'[29] Evgeniia Leonova called the film a mirror image of von Trier's *Dancer in the Dark*. 'The American viewer expects a happy end, but von Trier destroys his illusion. Muratova acts analogously' – i.e. she provides the Russo-Ukrainian viewer, used to unhappy endings, with an unexpected 'happy end', no matter how contrived. By following *Three Stories* with *Minor People*, Muratova repeated the pattern of *Asthenic Syndrome* and *Sentimental Policeman*, alternating a film with a black vision of humanity and society with a light comedy. In this, Leonova remarked, 'She is again ahead of her time', noting that the film began shooting before a rash of discussion by Russian film critics about the need for a kinder, gentler cinema (*dobroe kino*) after a post-Soviet decade of *chernukha* and gangster films.[30]

## *Chekhov's Motifs* [2002]

> Having seen [Chekhov's Motifs] how can you say that there's very little goodness in it? And what's in all those films that you watch from morning to night and from dawn to dusk? Where they shoot and kill people unceremoniously one after the other, where a kind word simply doesn't exist and you never meet a kind person.
>
> Kira Muratova[31]

*Chekhov's Motifs* could also be seen as Muratova's idiosyncratic response to the call for a kinder, gentler cinema. It is, she insists, 'a reassertion of simple moral values. It's a film about the family. About love. You understand, it's very important for me that in this family they all love each other despite the fact that they are very different, and are pulled in different directions, and they quarrel.'[32] Asked in 1998 about plans for her next project, Muratova replied, 'I have no plans. There are things that I like. For instance, Liudmila Petrushevskaia. But you don't feel like changing anything in them, and, probably, it's not worth touching them.'[33] Instead of Petrushevskaia's bleak stories about family life, Muratova turned to Chekhov.

*Chekhov's Motifs* is based on two of his early, lesser-known works – the short story 'Difficult People' ['Tiazhelye liudi', 1886] and the one-act drama *Tatiana Repina* (1889). In 1987 Muratova denied any influence of Chekhov, and in 1997 she still complained, 'I don't like Chekhov because of his melancholy, his cheerlessness.'[34] But her attitude had changed by 2000: 'For a long time I couldn't stand Chekhov. At first, in my youth, I adored him. I rejected him after I fell deeply in love with Tolstoy and Dostoevsky. His humour and his manner annoyed me … Now, rereading his humoresques I understand that they are works of genius.'[35] 'Difficult People' is one of those early humoresques, written for money when Chekhov was an impoverished medical student. It is set on a rural homestead, where the eldest son, preparing to return to his studies in the city, asks his skinflint father for money for the journey. His mother chimes in with a request to buy him some decent new trousers and boots, and the son hints he could do with some cash to support himself till he finds a job. The father explodes in anger, and the son stalks out of the house.

*Tatiana Repina* is Chekhov's least-known dramatic work. It was written in a single sitting, as a whimsical present to his friend and publisher Suvorin, whose four-act comedy of the same name had recently opened in both Russian capitals. Suvorin's play drew on an 1881 incident in which an actress poisoned herself on the stage of the Kharkov theatre; it was followed by several copycat suicides. Suvorin's Repina poisons herself after being jilted by her lover Sabinin, an impoverished landowner, society playboy and ladies' man, who is after the dowry of the rich and beautiful young widow Olenina. Chekhov's play depicts Sabinin and Olenina's wedding, during which the groom, traumatised by the appearance of a mysterious, moaning woman in the church, can barely get through the ceremony. Chekhov satirically counter-pointed the whispering and gossip of the wealthy guests with the otherworldly Slavonic liturgy chanted by the priests and choir. By the end, even the bride and groom are barely paying attention, and can scarcely wait for the ceremony to be over. Sending the play to Suvorin, Chekhov commented, 'It's cheaper than cheap. After you read it, you can throw it in the fireplace. Or even before.'[36] Muratova described *Tatiana Repina* as 'Not at all theatrical. I don't even know who would be able to cope with the task of staging it.'[37] Isolated from the theatrical world of Moscow, she did not know until told by an interviewer that Valeri Fokin had recently done so.[38] She understood the difficulty of staging a ceremony in which the guests, bride and groom stand in one position for nearly an hour facing the altar. The camera, she knew, provided possibilities for mobile points of view that the stage didn't allow.

The film is about both love and beauty, laced with Muratova's idiosyn-cratic humour, which keeps sentimentality at bay. Using a new cameraman, Valeri Makhnev, Muratova returned to black and white, recalling the aesthetic of *Brief Encounters* and *The Long Farewell* while adding to the Chekhovian atmosphere. Muratova commented, 'the black and white image makes every-thing alive and not alive more significant, more refined and more realistic at the same time.'[39] As always, she delighted in finding beauty in the commonplace, in the farmstead as well as the church wedding. She used the crisp detail of the black and white image to create a visual fugue of barnyard life: geese drinking, gliding across the bottom of the frame; pigs crowding together in a pen; chickens perching on the edge of a feeding bowl; a turkey cock, simultaneously magnificent and ludicrous. The music accompanying this delightful sequence is Silvestrov's hauntingly romantic melody from *Getting to Know the Big, Wide World*:

> The luminous thread of music stretches out
> Again forgotten days come to life.
> Spring carries us far, far away,
> When suddenly in the silence it sounds through the window.
> And again we live in a magical world
> And the distance is flooded with light,
> And again my childhood returns to me
> For ever, for ever, for ever.

This is not the only link between *Chekhov's Motifs* and Muratova's most sentimental film – she brought back Nina Ruslanova and Sergei Popov, who had played Liuba and Misha. That was also the only other time she filmed a wedding – albeit a Komsomol mass wedding. In the hour-long Orthodox wedding sequence of *Chekhov's Motifs*, the beauty is both visual (the church interior) and aural (the chanting of the liturgy).

Muratova said she was attracted not so much to Chekhov as to the locations: 'I'm always interested in the milieu in which the action will take place. I always want it to be new and fresh. I'm sick of cafés, cars, streets. The farm has gone out of fashion, so it's interesting...I don't remember anyone filming half of a movie in a church.'[40] *Chekhov's Motifs* opens in a rainy barnyard, where three carpenters are taking a lunch break. A boy of about seven, holding a baby goat, studies them solemnly, and they tease him, claiming they are building a pet food store rather than a shed. His five-year-old brother, in round-eyed glasses (all members of this family, except the baby, wear glasses), comes to stare. An extreme close-up focuses on the glasses of the father (Popov), kneeling by the pig pen and staring at a large pig, which stares back. The animals and children in the film provide Muratova with the kind of gentle visual humour not seen in her work since *The Sentimental Policeman*. In one hilarious sequence, the baby, sitting in a high chair at the table, nods off while his father is ranting about how the family is reducing him to penury.[41] As he gesticulates, the father knocks off his eyeglasses, which fly into a bowl of soup. Varia, the fey, cheeky twelve-year-old daughter, impishly fishes them out and sucks into her mouth a long noodle that has wrapped itself around them.

The central episode of the film's first section is the family dinner, staged for the camera like the Last Supper, with the family sitting on three sides of a long table. The domestic details of the interior are meaningful sociologically and emotionally. 'The house is furnished prettily and attractively. Lots of decorative towels embroidered with moralizing slogans and other touches of traditional village cosiness.'[42] The attractive china, lace-edged linens, the daughter's hand-knit sweater, the mother's carefully braided hairdo, all testify that this is a relatively prosperous family and the children are well cared for. At one point, father and son confront each other, framed symmetrically on either side of an elaborately framed icon. In the midst of the argument, Varia turns on the television and the mother watches the screen, spellbound by the beauty of Natalia Makarova performing the Saint-Saëns 'Dying Swan' solo made famous by ballerina Anna Pavlova. The performance echoes the elegant movements of the geese we saw earlier in the barnyard, just as the father's elaborate preening before dinner recalled the posturing of the turkey cock.

The life of the Russian clergy provides a tenuous link between the two Chekhov works. The father in 'Difficult People' is a priest's son who inherited land given to his father by the local noblewoman. In *Tatiana Repina*, the priests conduct the wedding ceremony and then, removing their robes, move back into everyday life. Church rituals and the personal life of the Orthodox clergy, for obvious reasons, were not shown in Soviet cinema. Muratova never displayed devotion to the Russian Orthodox church – if anything, her radical humanist views are closer to those of Tolstoy, whom the Church excommunicated. 'I'm not a believer. I'd very much like to believe, but I was raised differently. I simply place religion very high as a factor of culture, human history and morality.' But she confessed to a mad love for church singing.[43] One of the most significant lines of the film is put in the mouth of Kuzma, the sexton (Leonid Kushnir): 'Every day we marry, baptize, and bury them, and all to no purpose... And they sing, and they burn incense, and they read, and God still doesn't listen.'

In the wedding sequence, which occupies nearly an hour of the film, Muratova's attitude to the Church and its liturgy is respectful. Her broad satire is reserved for the wealthy guests and wedding couple, for whom traditional Orthodox rituals are simply another superficial affectation of their New Russian lifestyle. Vera, the bride, is played by Buzko, whose character in *Minor People* was also Vera, completing the traditional trio of names begun in Muratova's early films with heroines played by Ruslanova named Hope (Nadezhda/Nadia in *Brief Encounters*) and Love/Charity (Liubov/Liuba in *Getting to Know the Big, Wide World*). The hypothesis 'Nobody loves anyone', first uttered despairingly in *Getting to Know the Big, Wide World* by Ruslanova's Liuba, resurfaces in *Chekhov's Motifs* when Ruslanova, returning to Muratova's cinema after an absence of twenty years, congratulates the newly-weds in a bitter-sweet tone: 'I love it so much when somebody loves someone. Oh,

Verochka! Nobody loves anyone!' But, as Muratova kept insisting to the critics, there is love in this film, as well as humour.

Muratova always took liberties with her source texts: 'I long ago realized that it's easy for me to write on the basis of something I like and based on which I can fly far away ... And then to come back, spit on the whole thing, and make out of this little seed some sort of flourishes.'[44] But, in this film, she kept most of Chekhov's dialogue, often word for word; her flourishes were primarily visual. She simply updated the action: the farm family watches television, the son is picked up by a wedding guest in a late-model Toyota SUV. Muratova originally planned to project several quotations from Chekhov's narrator as intertitles, but these are not in the final version. Her most significant departure from *Tatiana Repina* is that the mysterious moaning woman in black is not, as in Chekhov, a friend of the late Tatiana seeking revenge but Father Ivan's rebellious daughter, bent on disrupting her father's service.

Chekhov's late nineteenth-century provincial landowners and theatrical bohemians translated easily into New Russians/New Ukrainians. The bride and many of the guests in the wedding scene were played by members of the popular Odessa-based comic troupe Maski-Show. Buzko is almost unrecognisable in her white gown, pale skin and exaggerated eye make-up, 'stylized as the suffering heroine of silent films'.[45] Another reviewer has described her

16. *Chekhov's Motifs*: Georgi Deliev, Natalia Buzko, Irina Doronina (photo credit: E. Golubenko)

as 'something between a clown and Pannochka [the beautiful dead witch in Gogol's folk/horror story "Vii"]',[46] still another as 'doll-like'.[47] Perhaps the unloved Vera is the culmination of Muratova's series of unloved dolls.

D. Saveliev observes that Muratova 'collects people and puts them in her celluloid album'.[48] Just as her non-professionals each brought their own narratives with them, her favourite actors brought to each new role the subtexts of their previous appearances, creating parallels and counterpoints. Almost every actor in the film had worked with Muratova before: Daniel in *Three Stories* and *Minor People*, Buzko in *Asthenic Syndrome*, *Three Stories* and *Minor People*, Kushnir in *The Sentimental Policeman* and *Three Stories*. Popov was making his fifth appearance in a Muratova film, Ruslanova her fourth. Panov, the Misha of *Minor People*, played the farmer's son, while his real-life mother played the mother.

Muratova filmed *Chekhov's Motifs* in two three-week shoots – in late November to early December 2001 on a farmstead not far from Odessa, and again in February in the church at Usatovo. The film was not ready for the Berliniale, but Muratova entered it in the Moscow Film Festival, which had fallen on hard times along with the Russian film industry. In the previous year not a single Russian-language film was entered in the competition. In 2002 there were several, of which *Chekhov's Motifs* and Rogozhkin's *Cookoo* [Kukushka] were seen as leading contenders. The sentimental *Cookoo*, with its anti-war, anti-nationalist message, was the audience favourite. To the surprise and dismay of critics and audience alike, the jury awarded the grand prize to Vittorio Taviani's television mini-series of Tolstoy's *Resurrection*. But the Moscow film critics, still Muratova's most loyal supporters, voted *Chekhov's Motifs* their Golden Elephant for best film. It was shown at the 2002 Karlovy Vary Festival, at the New York Festival of New Russian Cinema in October and at art museum venues in the United States, where viewers appreciated its gentle humour, if not its length. Muratova filmed the wedding ceremony nearly in its entirety in real time, forcing the viewer to experience the same impatience as the groom and the guests. Reviewing the film in *Iskusstvo kino*, Abdullaeva argues that 'Muratova has made time the central hero of this film'. She intentionally defies audience expectations, while expectation itself, particularly the expectation of an ending to the wedding ceremony, is one of the structural themes of the film.[49]

Reviews were generally enthusiastic. 'A brave creative experiment, dramatic and grotesque simultaneously ... one of the best films in Muratova's bio-graphy.'[50] 'Kira Muratova again demonstrated the virtuosity of her talent, but the jury noted the coldness and calculation of the director in the depiction of human weakness.'[51] Abdullaeva noted that Chekhov had tried out 'new forms' in the old dramatic canon by weaving together banal language, exalted dramatic elements and the comic. Muratova, she argues, intensified these Chekhovian motifs to the point of the grotesque, and it is actually Chekhov's experiments, rather than his texts, that interest her.[52] 'Accustomed to Kira Muratova's radicalism, we have stopped being astonished by her films. But *Chekhov's Motifs* flabbergasts us…The theatrical innovators of the last century turned, for the renewal of stage ideas, to the ritual forms of ancient theatre. Kira Muratova puts the early Chekhov on the screen and turns cinema into a ritual event.'

The film is about memory as well as time. By bringing back the black and white style of her first two films, Silvestrov's hauntingly nostalgic romance and beloved actors from the various periods of her work, Muratova has constructed a retrospective swansong. Now a grandmother just turned seventy, Muratova looks back over her career with pleasure and satisfaction, and invites us to do the same. But, ever the rebel, she challenges us to keep seeing the world in a new way.

Muratova, however, is still not ready to stop making films. In the autumn of 2003, she shot a new film in Odessa, a 'contemporary criminal melodrama' titled *The Tuner* [Nastroishchik]. It features Muratova's two favourite actresses, Ruslanova and Litvinova, Georgi Deliev, director of the 'eccentric' Maski-Show, and Alla Demidova, one of Russia's leading stage actresses, making her first appearance in a Muratova film. The plot is loosely based on the book *King of Detection*, the memoirs of the pre-Revolutionary detective Arkadi Koshko. As in *Chekhov's Motifs*, Muratova updates the action to the present day. It is being produced by the Pygmalion Studio, the website of which describes the film as 'an elegant psychological investigation of the motives that lead a refined intellectual conservatory student to work out a plan for appropriating the money of an elderly lady who adores him. This Raskolnikov of our time uses not an axe but contemporary computer technology to put his scheme into effect.' The script was written by Chetverkov with the participation of Golubenko and Muratova herself, and the filming took place on the streets of downtown Odessa. As this book went to press, it was scheduled to premiere at the Venice Film Festival in September 2004, and in New York in the winter of 2005.

Of her new film, Muratova said,

> It is a small, simple story about swindlers. Such is the main hero. He passes himself off as a tuner of musical instruments to gain entry into people's homes. And there's another pair of swindlers besides him. It is a film about victimhood, as I understand it. People want to give themselves up, they want to be robbed, used, and be useful in that way. They're ready to give up their soul, their body, their money. This is a touching quality, characteristic of very many of our fellow-citizens.

# 8. Afterwords

Muratova is the only director in her generation to live through the thaw, stagnation and perestroika with dignity, confounding those around her with her invincible creative spirit and anarchism of a somewhat Balkan persuasion.

Andrei Plakhov[1]

Kira Muratova, throughout her career, has been a truly independent film-maker – free of the pieties and stylistic clichés of Soviet cinema, free of the fads and pandering to mass taste of the post-Soviet era. Though she has won awards for 'defence of freedom', the freedom she is most concerned with is her own artistic independence. In Soviet times that concern became, of course, political, for the cultural watchdogs feared stylistic dissidence that might conceal hidden political messages.

For a director who was practically unknown until 1987 and has made only twelve feature-length films in her entire career, Kira Muratova has been the subject of a many critical essays and reviews, particularly in Russian. This is the first book on Muratova in a Western language, but there are already two in Russian.[2] Muratova, a difficult and challenging film-maker, is a film critic's dream – her films lend themselves to myriad interpretations, discussion and debate. Though she is somewhat reclusive in nature and dislikes interviews, she has been generous in giving them. She is extremely articulate about what she is trying to do in her art, particularly when the interviewer is knowledgeable about her work. Certain questions recur again and again, and her answers have remained unusually consistent over the years. I have often relied on Muratova's own words from interviews, including my own, to provide insight into her individual films. In this concluding chapter, I offer a selection of her more general comments on her art and her life. Admittedly, Muratova may have mixed feelings about this.

On interviews:

> I'm convinced that one doesn't need to know anything about the author and the director. It gets in the way. You should consider the finished product as it is...I don't like interviews. The best that I have to offer, the most interesting things, are in my films. All the rest is unnecessary ballast. (1990)[3]

On her art:

> I am an egotist; egotism is the essence of my métier. As a spectator, I love films of all styles and diverse origins. As a director, your opinions, that of the public, are not important to me. I want to construct my own world. (1988)[4]

> I love chance on principle and in all its forms. (1988)[5]

> I'm a conformist in life and a maximalist in art...Art is for me the kingdom of freedom of the soul. And here I want to be free to do what I choose...When I begin to make a film, I feel that I can kill the spirit of weight and rise into the heavens...I don't believe in God. I don't believe in anything supernatural. Because art is my religion. (1990)[6]

> Art in general shouldn't dress itself in the mantle of 'prophet, teacher of life'. (1990)[7]

> People in the film business are very coarse professionals, coarse, like surgeons. I would say: sometimes even like butchers...The cinema is a totally unnecessary thing, a luxury. And all art is a luxury. It is in no way obligatory. A luxury. Opium. A narcotic. So what? [...] And why should I make things that are necessary for people? (1995)[8]

> If I had said that I was filming not only at a cemetery but at a dog pound, then I would have heard from the administration: 'Get out of here!' So, naturally, I dissembled...The more prohibitions, the more imagery. Figurativeness in general grew entirely out of prohibitions, just as all art was born from prohibitions, shame and fear. (1995)[9]

> Play. A cat plays with a mouse before eating it. What is that play? It's theatre. It's an étude. When she's eaten enough, a thousand mice, and begins to play with a piece of paper...that's art in nature. (1991)[10]

> I love this profession. It's not that I love it, I adore it. It's a form of existence, which has been installed in me like a program in a computer. It's my narcotic, my life. I'm a director for myself. (1995)[11]

> I love my films. I feel protected around them, like a mother among her own children...The gloomiest thing, if it's well done, leaves the impression of joy. That's creativity. That doesn't mean that I don't love life or I love death. It's another thing that death interests me. (1997)[12]

> Harmony doesn't mean balance. You must destroy something symmetrically, break rules. It's only then that things grab you. (1997)[13]

> Freedom is only when you're shooting something. You think – oh, I'm flying about, I'm a moth, no rules of the road apply to me, no laws of gravity. I have no children, let everyone go to ...I don't have to wash anything, cook anything. I'm free!!! (1998)[14]

We feel pleasure and pain with the same nerve, however, as a rule it protects itself during one's lifetime, and eventually a callus grows over it. It becomes less sensitive: 'Don't disturb me, I want to sleep tight.' It is as if I painfully scrape off the calluses so that at last I can anoint it with oil... It is a contrast of torture and pleasure. (1998)[15]

## On repetition:

Repetition – that's my mania – haven't you noticed? Those endless repetitions are from a desire to rhyme, a desire for a kind of refrain. (1991)[16]

Q: There's the impression that you're bored with words, or why else in your films would dialogues be repeated to the point of senselessness?
M: That's simply because I love opera. How is it, after all, in opera? He sings, 'How I love you! How strongly I love you!' And she answers: 'The moon is shining! The moon is shining!' Chorus. (1997)[17]

## On her audience:

Sometimes someone will say: 'This is an entertaining film,' and you'll relax watching it. And I go and watch it and I experience an interminable and unrelieved boredom. Someone is entertained by it? So be it. I need a different game, a different entertainment – the play of the mind. That's also its own sort of entertainment. (1991)[18]

Every director would like to be understood by all and have every one like him – like Charlie Chaplin. And at the same time to be himself. I, unfortunately, rarely manage to combine these two opposite poles, these two forms of existence, but I would like to. (1992)[19]

I don't belong to the directors who can please a large number of viewers. I belong to the directors who can please a small, even very small, quantity of viewers, but please them very strongly. (1995)[20]

I might want to please everyone, but, before anything, I must please myself... My films are liked very much by a very few. (1999)[21]

## On film critics:

I salute the fact that people write about me and study my films. But this isn't really very necessary to me. I think, probably, the person finds his own interest in doing that. (1996)[22]

[Asked about rumours of a romance with Litvinova, or with Vysotsky]: I love it when they say something amusing about me. Why not? Perhaps. [...] I've begun to feel like food for film critics... They have to write about something, after all. (1998)[23]

It's just as interesting for me to read negative as positive reviews. I like something unusual, intelligent, interesting, like what Mikhail Yampolsky, for example, writes. But I don't have time for run-of-the-mill stuff. (1999)[24]

The most interesting is not when they praise you or criticize you, but when they construct their own conception of the film, and you see it all in a different way... I love and often film eccentrics, and among film critics there are very many who seem to me amusing and strange eccentrics. That's why I read all of this with interest. It's also play of the mind. (1999)[25]

## On love for humanity:

I can love a concrete man, not 'people'...There is the concept of 'humanity' but not of 'dogdom', 'cathood', or 'birdkind', which are much closer to me and to whom I feel much more responsible...I understand my responsibility for my own children and grandchildren, and also for animals, which mankind has domesticated. As for 'the people' [*narod*] I am the same people as others, and I don't owe it anything, and it doesn't owe me. (1996)[26]

There's no progress. There's a movement in circles. In that is all the beauty and tragedy of civilization. (1997)[27]

## On eccentrics and marginality:

I don't like to socialize with people in the world of the arts. I like to associate with eccentrics, strange, obsessed people. (1990)[28]

I don't know anything, I live in my own lair. I don't know what the audience wants, and I don't owe them anything. I want to do what I want to do, truthfully, to the end, expressing my attitude to everything around me, in me, and next to me. (1991)[29]

I'm unusually fond of those who somehow don't fit in to the world...all sorts of originals and kind nonconformists. Evil eccentrics bore me. (1997)[30]

In Odessa, there's a lack of information. I see films only at festivals. (1997)[31]

My cinema in part consists of those people who wouldn't understand my films. (1997)[32]

The man who told the story of the snake in *Asthenic Syndrome* really was mentally ill, and he wanted to be filmed saying all that. (1998)[33]

## On her actors:

For me, the actor is only a component of the shot...On what principle do I usually choose actors for a picture? [...] I look at an actor not from the position that he's an actor...no – I'm interested in the way he behaves, what there is interesting in him. How he sits, how he smokes, how he walks, becomes embarrassed, how he's introduced to me for the first time. I try to calculate in him something not of the actor but purely of the human being, that which can be used one time. In a film, let's say. That is, I look at an actor – pardon me – as typage. (1991)[34]

Chance is productive for me...Let's say Sasha Svenskaia lives across from the studio. She was filmed as an extra. Sasha is an elevator operator – more than that – she works as a janitor, trades at the market...I love eccentrics. Usually they are either strange or ugly. But Renata [Litvinova], while a real eccentric by her psychological organization, is also a beauty. (1997)[35]

Renata in some sense is mad, she's a holy fool. (1997)[36]

[Renata], like Seryozha [Popov], first made an impression with her text, then her personality...Someone gave me something of his. I read it. I met him and then decided I wanted to film him. It was the same with Renata. (1999)[37]

Ruslanova? If I hadn't discovered her, then in five minutes someone else would have. She was such a striking person. (1999)[38]

On her own life:

I'm not an Odessite. I came here by chance and I stay here…Biologically, I'm a healthy organism with an optimistic nature. (1997)[39]

Can you say what your daughter does? No – [sigh] – she's an addict. That's ninety percent of my life. (1998)[40]

When you have children, difficult children, you get scared; there's no money, how are we going to live? I believe that monsters like me should be sterilized. They should not be allowed to reproduce since they are incapable of providing for their children. (1998)[41]

I consider myself not a very sociable person, with a tendency to isolation, hermit-like, perhaps…I had just such a childhood, but that feeling intensified, because I've made myself a very sociable directing style…People come up to me on the street and say, 'I want to be in your films.' I try it out – could we take him for this role, or think up some role for him? (1999).[42]

You know, I never have enough time to be alone, thus I can't say that loneliness is bad. I love solitude and my whole life I've not had enough of it…[At VGIK] I didn't suffer from solitude, on the contrary. I didn't socialize with others, with other departments, for example. I lived in the dormitory…I didn't like to go visiting, and I still don't like sitting around a table…I never drank, you understand…I didn't understand what I thought was empty, friendly talk. Those conversations, perhaps, are not empty, but they always seemed boring to me…I don't like to talk about art, or about cinema, In general I don't find it pleasurable to talk. Perhaps only on very specific, limited, focused subjects, with precise people who interest me, who know more about that subject than I do. (1999)[43]

I never have enough time to do the things I want to do. To do what I want, I need a lot of solitude and concentration. Even to concentrate takes time. No one can distract me. But all the time I'm distracted by everyday, family burdens, which I'm obliged to carry. I have a very strong sense of duty, which is highly developed and weighs on me. I have family obligations to the children. I love my child and I have no other choice…I don't have enough time to simply think, write, to do what I most want to do. I always am obliged to be doing something else…I would need a lot of money to hire servants, a nanny, so they would do all of that, and so I could live, so to speak, in my own world. But it's worked out that I don't have money. That means I don't have time for solitude. (1999)[44]

I'm not very interested in film makers like myself. I'm interested instead in what was not given to me, what I don't know how to do myself. (1999)[45]

In 1999 Muratova was awarded the prestigious prize of the Berlin Festival of the Arts. Film scholar Hans-Joachim Schlegel wrote in his citation:

Kira Muratova, with unshakeable courage, overcoming all obstacles, sought her own place, relying on her inborn, individual, uncompromising artistic gift. She found her place and resists all temptations, in particular the imposition of others' ideas…

Kira Muratova's films are full of provocations, they attempt to shatter the petrification of our feelings and imagination. She treats the traditional belief in the power of art, in its ability to transform or even to improve the world, with a deep scepticism and mocking irony. And nevertheless in her provocation and ironic play there is always the chance of liberation – through shock therapy.[46]

The following year, at the Berliniale, Muratova was awarded the Andrzej Wajda Freedom Prize, named after its first laureate. When Wajda himself presented the award, Muratova replied:

I feel like a marginal person who has crawled out of a dark sewer into the light, blinded by the light. It turns out my work is necessary. Such encounters give me strength to work on new projects. In practical life I am not a fighter. I live like everyone else. But art is the kingdom of freedom. And I serve this kingdom.[47]

# Notes

## Chapter 1

1   A. Zorkii, 'Beleet parus odinokii', *Sovetskii ekran*, no. 8, 1987, p.15.
2   Author's telephone interview with Muratova, October 2001.
3   B. Bollag, M. Ciment, 'Entretien avec Kira Muratova', *Positif*, no. 324, 1986, p.9.
4   She was at one time the Deputy Minister of Health for Maternal and Child Health.
5   E. Tarkhanova, 'Chrezvychaino mnogo dobra', *MK Bul'var'*, no. 29, 15 July 2002.
6   L. Arkus et al. (eds), *Noveishaia istoriia otechestvennogo kino 1986–2000*, Part I, Kinoslovar', vol. 2, St Petersburg, 2001, p.297.
7   E. Zhenin, 'Kira Muratova: Zhanne d'Ark prosto nravilos' goret' na kostre', *Ekran i stsena*, 5 December 1991, p.14.
8   S.I. Iutkevich et al., *Kino: Entsiklopedicheskii slovar'*, Moscow, 1986, p.93.
9   Author's interview with Natal'ia Riazantseva, Moscow, January 2001.
10  A. Muratov, 'Zhizn' moia, ili ty prisnilas' mne?', *Renessans*, no. 15, 1997, p.14.
11  Bollag and Ciment, 'Entretien', p.9.
12  According to Grigorii Kunitsyn, a Central Committee culture specialist at the time, Ukrainian party authorities fired several film studio officials for approving the film. He had it shown to Khrushchev, who liked it, and Kiev rescinded the firings. W. Taubman, *Khrushchev: The Man and His Era*, New York, 2003, p.600.
13  M. Veksler, 'Interview with Muratova' in E. Gromov (ed.), *Kira Muratova '98*, Moscow (VGIK), 1999, p.76.
14  A. Getmanchuk, 'Kira Muratova: Pravda vsegda shokiruet', *Komsomol'skaia pravda*, no. 127, 2 June 1990. According to Aleksandra Sviridova (author's interview, New York, 2001) the studio's sympathetic director created the museum to provide employment for Muratova.
15  F. Navailh, 'Kira Mouratova ou l'insoutenable lucidité de l'être', *Cinéma*, no. 34, 23 March 1988, p.16.
16  V. Katanian, *Paradjanov. Tsena vechnogo prazdnika*, Nizhny Novgorod, 2001, p.234.
17  N. Zlobina, L. Karasev, 'Otkrytiia i paradoksy: Zametki o tvorchestve K. Muratovoi i A. Germana', *Literaturnoe obozrenie*, no. 2, 1988, p.78.

18  Boris Vladimirsky, an Odessa intellectual who knew her well, titled a profile of Muratova '...Kotoraia guliala sama po sebe' ('...Who walked alone'); *Vecherniaia Odessa*, 23 May 1989.
19  Bollag and Ciment, 'Entretien', p.9.
20  Arkus et al. (eds), Part II, *Kino i Kontekst, 1986–1988*, vol. 4, pp.70–71.
21  D. Bykov, 'Kira Muratova: Chto-to drugoe', *Literaturnaia gazeta*, 16 December 1992, p.8.
22  Author's interview with Muratova, Moscow, April 1991.
23  L. Farrah, 'Soviets Unshelved', *Films and Filming*, no. 408, September 1988, p.17.
24  Getmanchuk, 'Pravda'.
25  'Three Soviet Film Makers Take Their Work on Tour', *The New York Times*, 20 September 1989, p.C34.
26  V. Bozhovich, *Kira Muratova: Tvorcheskii portret*. Moscow, 1988, p.3. Most, but not all, of the material in this hard-to-find short book is contained in Bozhovich's article, 'Rentgenoskopiia dushi', *Iskusstvo kino*, no. 8, April 1987, pp.14–15.
27  Bollag and Ciment, 'Entretien', p.9.
28  A. Plakhov, 'Kira Muratova: Mne nuzhna lozhka degtia', *Kommersant*, 4 November 1998, p.10.
29  Bollag and Ciment, 'Entretien', p.11.
30  Bozhovich, *Kira Muratova*, p.18.
31  Plakhov, *Vsego tridtsat' tri: zvezdy mirovoi kinorezhissury*, Vinnitsa, 1999, pp.199–212.

**Chapter 2**

1  I. Shilova, 'V poiskakh utrachennoi liubvi', *Kinostsenarii*, no. 2, 1989, p.186.
2  S.I. Iutkevich et al., *Kino*, p.264.
3  Plakhov, 'Kinematograf v podpol'e', *Strana i mir*, no. 1, 1991, p.156.
4  Shilova, 'V poiskakh', pp.186–187.
5  J. Woll, *Real Images: Soviet Cinema and the Thaw*, London, 2000, pp.194–195. I. Shilova, 'Cherno-beloe kino', *Kinovedcheskie zapiski*, no. 32, 1996/7, pp.25–37.
6  Muratova interview, 1991.
7  Muratova has never named the actress in any published interview. The only other filmed performance by Muratova I have been able to locate is a small part in the film *Dangerous Tour* [Opasnye gastroli, 1969], also featuring Vysotsky, directed by G. Yungval'd-Khil'kevich.
8  Bozhovich, *Kira Muratova*, p.7.
9  Muratova interview, 1991.
10  V. Gul'chenko, 'Mezhdu ottepeliami', *Iskusstvo kino*, no. 6, 1991, p.61.
11  Bozhovich, *Kira Muratova*, p.5. She commented to French interviewers that, having lived quite comfortably in Romania, she was incredulous that a major city could exist with such an irregular water and sewage system. Bollag and Ciment, 'Entretien', p.9.
12  Muratova interview, 1991.
13  Author's interview with Leonid Zhukhovitsky, Moscow, January 2001.
14  Lev Anninskii, *Shestidesiatniki i my*, Moscow, 1991, p.220.
15  N. Kovarskii, 'Chelovek i vremia', *Iskusstvo kino*, no. 10, 1968, p.56.
16  I. Izvolova, 'Zvuk lopnuvshei struny', *Iskusstvo kino*, no. 8, 1998, p.111.
17  Izvolova, 'Zvuk', p.113.

18   Anninskii, *Shestidesiatniki*, p.221.
19   According to Woll, p.219, 'Only eight million viewers saw *Wings* in 1966, though film critics nearly unanimously chose Bulgakova as best actress of 1966'. Khutsiev chose a similar heroine for *July Rain* [Iul'skii dozhd', 1966]; although in her late twenties, she decides not to marry a prestigious intelligentsia suitor.
20   Muratova interview, 1991.
21   Zorkii, 'Beleet parus odinokii', *Sovetskii ekran*, no. 8, April 1987, pp.14–15.
22   Bozhovich, *Kira Muratova*, p.8.
23   Plakhov, *Vsego 33*, p.207.
24   Gromov (ed.), *Kira Muratova '98*, pp.185–187.
25   The screenplay was published in *Kinostsenarii*, no. 1, 1988, pp.136–153, with a preface 'Za chto?' by Riazantseva, discussing the censorship difficulties encountered by both the screenplay and the film.
26   Zarkhi was the head of the division. His note is quoted in V.I. Fomin, *Polka: Dokumenty. Svidetel'stva. Kommentarii*, Moscow, 1992, p.93. Fomin devotes an entire chapter (pp.92–109) to the shelving of *The Long Farewell*, on which much of the following discussion is based.
27   Riazantseva, 'Za chto?', p.138.
28   Muratova interview, 1991.
29   A. Sviridova, 'Kira Muratova: Eto moi narkotik, moia zhizn'', *Novoe russkoe slovo*, 15 May 1995.
30   F. Sabouraud, 'Éloge de la ténacité: entretien avec Kira Muratova', *Cahiers du Cinéma*, no. 402, December 1987, p.37.
31   Izvolova, 'Zvuk', p.118.
32   Izvolova, 'Zvuk', p.119.
33   Shilova, 'V poiskakh', p.188.
34   Plakhov, *Vsego 33*, p.207.
35   *The New York Times*, 14 April 1995.
36   In the Soviet Union, Lermontov's novel was part of the required literature curriculum in the eighth class. Since Muratova finished the final three years of her school in Romania, she escaped the traditional pedagogical treatment of the work.
37   Bozhovich, *Kira Muratova*, p.13.
38   Zorkii, 'Beleet', p.14.

**Chapter 3**

1   V. Matizen, 'Zhenshchina, kotoroi skuchen alfavitnyi poriadok' (www. film.ru/ article.asp?ID=2645).
2   Bollag and Ciment, 'Entretien', p.11.
3   Shilova, 'V poiskakh', p.188.
4   Z. Abdullaeva, 'Propushchennyi avangard', *Iskusstvo kino*, no. 8, 1994, pp.88–91.
5   Plakhov, *Vsego 33*, p.208. The artists Komar and Melamid invented the term 'sots-art' in the mid-1970s, and are its best-known exemplars. Sots-art parodies the style and clichés of Socialist Realist art.
6   Bozhovich, *Kira Muratova*, p.15.
7   Discussion of the Film *Getting to Know the Big, Wide World, Kadr*, Lenfilm Studio newsletter, 13 October 1978. Translated in V. Golovskoy, *Behind the Soviet Screen:*

*The Motion Picture Industry in the USSR 1972–1982*, Ann Arbor, 1986, pp.124–126. All excerpts from the discussion in this paragraph are from this source.

8    M. Trofimenkov, 'Poznavaia belyi svet', *Seans*, no. 8, 1994, p.61.

9    'Annotatsiia', in *Poznavaia belyi svet: montazhnaia zapis' khudozhestvennogo fil'ma*, Moscow, 1980, p.55. These 'montazhnye listy' were published in small editions for the benefit of film critics and translators. They contained an exact transcription of the dialogue, annotations of music on the soundtrack, and a description of the length and camera placement for each shot.

10   'Shelestiat na vetru beriozy', *Iskusstvo kino*, no. 5, 1977, pp.167–191.

11   Muratova interview, 1991.

12   Zlobina and Karasev, 'Otkrytiia', p.79.

13   Shilova, 'V poiskakh', p.188.

14   Shilova, 'V poiskakh', p.188.

15   I am grateful to Inna Andreevna Babyonysheva for this information.

16   There is one brief mention by Jean that 'Pan Valentin' knows Latin.

17   Telephone interview with Muratova, 2001.

18   Bollag and Ciment, 'Entretien', p.11.

19   E. Stishova, 'Poznavaia belyi svet', *Iskusstvo kino*, no. 11, 1999, p.88. There is an interesting parallel here with the work of Liudmila Petrushevskaia, who in the 1990s became increasingly active as an amateur painter and watercolourist. She produced a series of watercolour studies of dolls with flower bouquets and other objects, emphasising the dolls' beauty but eerie lifelessness.

20   Bollag and Ciment, 'Entretien', p.11.

21   Bozhovich, *Kira Muratova*, p.18.

22   Navailh, 'Parmi les pierres grises', *Cinéma*, no. 441, May 1988, p.21.

23   M.V., 'Kira Muratova Slavissimo', *Cinéma*, no. 441, May 1988, p.21.

24   L.C., 'Sredi serikh kamnei', *Positif*, nos. 329–330, July–August 1988, p.85.

25   J.M. Frodon, 'Kira Muratova: l'oeuvre mutilée', *Le point*, no. 818, 23 May 1988, p.72.

26   Telephone interview with Muratova, 2001.

27   Plakhov, *Vsego 33*, p.208.

28   Muratova interview, 1991. The introductory annotation to the dialogue lists by editor N. Nekrasova still maintains a traditional Soviet interpretation: 'The authors of the film have tried to study the relationships of people within the traditional love "triangle" in the conditions of sanctimonious, hypocritical bourgeois society, where falsehood beneath the mask of decency corrupts and deforms human beings.'

29   According to Plakhov, it was filmed in Isfara, Tadzhikistan.

30   Plakhov, 'Peremena dekoratsii', *Iskusstvo kino*, no. 7, 1988, p.45.

31   Susan Larsen, acknowledging the obvious Freudian symbolism, gives a nuanced reading of Filip's fascination with the beauty, not the purpose, of guns in 'Encoding Difference: Figuring Gender and Ethnicity in Kira Muratova's *A Change of Fate*', in N. Condee (ed.), *Soviet Hieroglyphics: Visual Culture in Late Twentieth-Century Russia*, Bloomington and London, 1995, p.122.

32   I quote the excellent translation on p.115 of Larsen's 'Encoding Difference'. Larsen gives a persuasive reading of the film from the perspective of Laura Mulvey's theory of the male gaze and theorists of orientalism, including Edward Said and Homi Bhabha. On p.118 she cites this monologue as evidence of the film's 'coding of racial difference in terms of gender'.

33   Muratova interview, 1991.
34   Plakhov, 'Peremena', p.41.
35   A. Shpagin, 'Krai', *Iskusstvo kino*, no. 2, 1991, p.28.
36   Shilova, 'V poiskakh', pp.189–190.

**Chapter 4**

1   Vladimirskii, 'Ne teriaite otchaianie', *Zerkalo*, no. 6, 1990.
2   Plakhov, 'Kinematograf', p.156.
3   L. Gersova, 'Kira Muratova otvechaet zriteliam', *Kinovedcheskie zapiski*, no. 13, 1992, p.160.
4   '*Soviet Film* presents a new film by Kira Muratova: *The Asthenic Syndrome*', *Soviet Film*, March 1990, p.6.
5   L. Paikova, 'Prut'ia mednoi kletki', *Literaturnoe obozrenie*, no. 3, 1991, p.89.
6   Serafima Roll analyses the connection between the film's structure and its meaning. 'The presence of two thematically different scenarios and two different protagonists who loosely organize the cinematic material around themselves deconstructs traditional semantic homogeneity of discourse, its closure, dominance of signifieds, and single point of view. Moreover, the presentation of the thematically disconnected episodes not only ruptures the smooth surface of representation but also prevents the articulation of a univocal ideological position.' 'Fragmentation and Ideology in Kira Muratova's *The Asthenic Syndrome* and Arto Paragamian's *Because Why*', *Canadian Journal of Film Studies*, vol. 5, no. 1, 1996, p.53.
7   Plakhov, 'Kinematograf', p.156.
8   Gersova, p.157.
9   For a discussion of this issue, mentioning Muratova's pioneering role, see Andrei Zorin, 'Legalizatsiia obtsennoi leksiki', in Gregory Freidin (ed.), *Russian Culture in Transition*, California Slavic Studies, vol. 7, 1993, p.143 n.38.
10   Getmanchuk, 'Pravda'.
11   D. Bykov, 'Kira Muratova nauchila Vysotskogo khripet'', *Profil'*, no. 9, 11 March 1997.
12   Telephone interview with Muratova, 2001. This has been incorrectly reported in some sources, leading me to state it incorrectly in an earlier work.
13   F. Audé, 'Faire voir, refléter, rien de plus', *Positif*, no. 363, May 1991, p.12.
14   Muratova actually invented this episode for a diploma screenplay many years earlier. Bykov, 'Nauchila'.
15   Audé, 'Faire voir', p.12.
16   Gersova, p.158.
17   Gersova, p.158. Ellen Berry similarly argues that 'The film acts as a provocation, a form of shock treatment or social psychotherapy, a call to action'. 'Grief and Simulation in Kira Muratova's *The Asthenic Syndrome*', *The Russian Review*, vol. 57, no. 3, July 1998, p.448.
18   Getmanchuk, 'Pravda'.
19   Bozhovich, 'Kira Muratova: I make films about what is in me', *Soviet Film*, March 1990, p.19.
20   N. Morozova, 'Kira Muratova: Fikus – eto rastenie. I ne bolee togo', *Sovetskaia molodezh*', 24 October 1990, pp.4–5.

21   J. Graffy, 'Conflict resolution', *Index on Censorship*, no. 3, 1990, p.24.
22   Graham Roberts discusses these two scenes in 'Look Who's Talking: the Politics of Representation and the Representation of Politics in Two Films by Kira Muratova', *Elementa*, no. 3, 1997, p.320. 'Rather than limit herself to a study of the politics of the gaze in cinema, however, Muratova also emphasizes the significance of the look – the visual image – in society at large.'
23   M. Topaz, 'O chernoi pechali i zvukakh truby', *Kino* (Riga), no. 7, 1990.
24   Vladimirsky himself often played that role in Odessa's cultural life in the 1980s.
25   German's *Trial on the Road* [Proverka na dorogakh, 1971, released 1986] and *My Friend Ivan Lapshin* [Moi drug Ivan Lapshin, 1982, released 1985] suffered shelving, as did Muratova's early films. Sokurov's difficult films, particularly his idiosyncratic version of Flaubert's *Madame Bovary, Save and Protect* [Spasi i sokhrani, 1989] were unpopular with Soviet censors and mass audiences alike.
26   Vladimirskii, 'Ne teriaite'.
27   Shooting script.
28   Gersova, p.163.
29   Gersova, p.165.
30   Audé, 'Fair voir', p.14.
31   'Christianity doesn't interest me. I am an atheist, or rather, a Tolstoyan.' Morozova, 'Fikus'.
32   Morozova, 'Fikus'.
33   Muratova discovered Svenskaia working as an elevator operator at the building across from the Odessa Studio. She originally cast her as Ivnikov's mother, then combined two roles and made her the vice-principal as well. She added her trumpet solo when she discovered that Svenskaia was also an amateur musician.
34   Gersova, p.159.
35   M.Yampolsky, 'In Defence of Somnolence', *Soviet Film*, no. 6, 1990, p.6.
36   Gersova, p.158.
37   Audé, 'Faire voir', p.14.
38   Morozova, 'Fikus'.
39   Yampolsky, 'In Defence', pp.6–7.
40   A. Timofeevskii, 'Urodlivaia roza', *Ekran i stsena*, 8 February 1990, p.5.
41   'Diagnoz: *Astenicheskii sindrom*: dokumenty, tsitaty bez kommentariev', *Ekran i stsena*, 11 January 1990, p.10. This and other documents that follow relating to the film's release were published by this journal.
42   Bozhovich, '"Asthenia" or what's wrong with us?', *Moscow News*, no. 44, 1989, p.11.
43   'Tupik? Chto meshaet vykhodu novogo fil'ma Kiry Muratovoi', *Komsomol'skaia pravda*, 10 December 1989.
44   L. Danielou, 'Nouvelles de glasnost', *Cahiers du cinéma*, no. 426, December 1989, p.13.
45   'Pole brani', *Komsomol'skaia pravda*, 22 December 1989. With his letter to the editor, Kamshalov enclosed a transcript of those expressions, 'which I simply can't bring myself to cite on a piece of paper bearing the letterhead of a state organization', and challenged the newspaper to print it alongside his reply. They did not dare.
46   F. Strauss, 'Kira Muratova', *Cahiers du cinéma*, no. 430, 1990, p.7.
47   K. Shcherbakov, 'Ulybka Kabirii?', *Iskusstvo kino*, no. 9, 1990, pp.146–147.
48   T. Khlopliankina, 'Shok', *Literaturnaia gazeta*, 14 February 1990, p.8.

49   N. Riazantseva, '*Astenicheskii sindrom* Kiry Muratovoi', *Sovetskii ekran*, no. 3, 1990, p.10.
50   D. Popov, 'Bog umer', *Iskusstvo kino*, no. 3, 1990, p.38.
51   See Navailh, 'Mouratova la survivante', *Cinéma*, no. 466, April 1990, pp.9–10; S. Bodrov, B. Bollag, 'Pathologie de la vie contemporaine', *Positif*, no. 351, May 1990, pp.50–51; F. Strauss, 'Kira Muratova', *Cahiers du cinéma*, no. 430, 1990, p.7; H.J. Rother, 'Genügt es, Tolstoi zu lesen?', *Film und Ferhsehen*, vol. 18, no. 7, July 1990, pp.25–27; B. Ben Sadoun, 'No Future?', *24 images*, vol. 24, nos. 50–51, autumn 1990; T. Jousse, 'K.O. technique', *Cahiers du cinéma*, no. 442, 1991, pp.61–62; R. Bassan, 'Le syndrome asthénique dans la tourmente de la perestroïka', *La Revue du cinéma*, April 1991, p.35; F. Audé, 'L'oeuvre et le chaos', *Positif*, no. 363, May 1991, pp.9–11.
52   Graffy, 'Conflict', p.24.
53   J. Downie, 'Kira Muratova, *The Asthenic Syndrome*', *Illusions*, June 1991, pp.19–20.
54   Plakhov, 'Kinematograf', p.156.
55   Vladimirskii, 'Ne teriaite'.

**Chapter 5**

1    C. Taboulay, 'Entretien avec Kira Muratova', *Cahiers du cinéma*, no. 442, April 1991, p.60.
2    For a discussion of Muratova's four films of the 1990s as cinema of the absurd see G. Roberts, 'The Meaning of Death: Kira Muratova's Cinema of the Absurd', in B. Beumers (ed.) *Russia on Reels: The Russian Idea in Post-Soviet Cinema*, London and New York, 1999, pp.144–160.
3    Bykov, 'Chto-to'.
4    Petrushevskaia's stories and plays are about contemporary Russian family life. Though there are elements of the grotesque in many of her stories, her work is generally closer to the 'hyper-realism' that characterises much of Muratova's work in cinema. Underlying all Petrushevskaia's work is a profound concern for the plight of the family and of single mothers in contemporary Russia. The two contemporaries and acquaintances once considered collaborating on a film project. In 1992 Muratova said, 'I'm reading Petrushevskaia's latest short novel [*The Time: Night*], and I'm laughing from enjoyment. Although everything there is terrible, of course, but it's done very well, and that's always fun.' Bykov, 'Chto-to'.
5    Gromov (ed.), *Kira Muratova '98*, p.72.
6    Taboulay, 'Entretien', p.60.
7    A. Kolodizhner, 'Kira Muratova: Ia prel'stilas' sladkimi rechami, no menia soblaznili i obmanuli', *Seans*, no. 9, 1994, p.40.
8    Author's interview with E. M. Vasil'eva, Amherst, MA, September 1991.
9    'Iskusstvo – eto utekha, otrada, i opium', *Iskusstvo kino*, no. 7, 1992, p.13.
10   See the reviews by F. Sabouraud, *Cahiers du Cinéma*, no. 222, May, 1993, pp.120–122; A. Kieffer, *Jeune Cinéma*, no. 222, May–June 1993, pp.49–50; and F. Audé, *Positif*, nos. 389–390, July–August 1993, p.26.
11   Muratova interview, 1991.
12   E. Zhenin, *Odesskii vestnik*, no. 19 (357), 29 January 1993.
13   T. Iskantseva, 'Sindrom Kiry Muratovoi', *Kuranty*, 4 March 1992.
14   L. Fomina, 'I militsionery liubit' umeiut', *Moskovskaia pravda*, 20 March 1992.

15   Muratova interview, 1991.
16   See Chapter 3, note 5.
17   Anninskii, 'Utochnenie diagnoza?', *Literaturnaia gazeta*, 1 April 1992.
18   V. Matizen, 'Povtorenie kak mat Chuvstvitel'nogo militsionera', *Seans*, no. 9, 1994, p.38.
19   T. Moskvina, 'Kira Muratova', in Arkus, *Kinoslovar'*, vol. 2. p.298.
20   S. Eisenstein, 'Montage of Attractions', in R. Taylor (ed.), *The Eisenstein Reader*, London, 1998, pp.29–34.
21   This non-diegetic strip of light was borrowed from religious paintings, according to Richard Taylor in *The Battleship Potemkin: the Film Companion*, London and New York, 2000, p.44.
22   K. Clark, 'Aural Hieroglyphics?: Some Reflections on the Role of Sound in Recent Russian Films and Its Historical Context', in N. Condee (ed.), *Soviet Hieroglyphics*, p.17.
23   Clark, 'Hieroglyphics?', p.17.
24   B. Kuz'minskii, 'Odesskii melovoi krug', *Nezavisimaia gazeta*, 25 March 1992.
25   Bozhovich even asserts they will never have a child of their own. 'Iz zhizni fantomov', *Iskusstvo kino*, no. 7, 1992, p.16.
26   Muratova interview, 1991.
27   Roberts stresses the importance of chance as an element of the absurd in Muratova's films from *Asthenic Syndrome* to *Three Stories*. He points in particular to this exchange.
28   Muratova interview, 1991.
29   See E. Tarkhanova, 'Vospitannoe smiatenie chuvstvitel'noi Kiry Muratovoi', *Kinovedcheskie zapiski*, no. 27, 1995, pp.51–69.
30   Besides three reviews by Bozhovich, Shepotinnik and Gul'chenko in *Iskusstvo kino*, no. 7, 1992, and others already cited, see those by E. Shur in *Komsomol'skaia pravda*, 24 February 1992; P. Arkad'ev in *Vecherniaia Moskva*, 3 June 1992; A. Shemiakin in *Arsenal*, no. 6, 1992; and A. Timofeevskii in *Moskovskie novosti*, 4 May 1992.
31   Kolodizhner, 'Ia prel'stilas'.
32   Plakhov, 'Legkaia muza, ili esteticheskii sindrom', *Iskusstvo kino*, no. 8, 1994, p.4.
33   Gromov (ed.), *Kira Muratova '98*, pp.65–66.
34   Gromov (ed.), *Kira Muratova '98*, p.66.
35   Bykov, 'Kira Muratova: "Ia ne koshka i ne Gospod" Bog', *Stolitsa*, no. 20, 1994, p.48.
36   Moskvina, 'Femina Sapiens', *Iskusstvo kino*, no. 4, 1998, p.47.
37   K. Priannik, 'Sladkaia privychka ubivat', *Moskovskii komsomolets*, 8 May 1998, p.11. For Litvinova's version of their first meeting, see I. Pospelova, 'Femme Fatale', *Domovoi*, no. 7 (11), 1994, p.73.
38   Bykov, 'Ia ne koshka', p.49.
39   A. Kriukova, 'Davali by snimat' fil'my', *Nezavisimaia gazeta*, 5 May 1994.
40   Plakhov, 'Legkaia muza', p.5.
41   Gromov (ed.), *Kira Muratova '98*, pp.66–67. Litvinova's monologues were published as 'Monologi medsestry' in *Kinostsenarii*, no. 5, pp.117–121. Two of them also appeared in *Iskusstvo kino*, no. 8, 1994, pp.12–13.
42   Fortunately, this film is available on DVD (Ruscico), which does justice to the colour photography.
43   Plakhov, 'Legkaia muza', p.4.

44    I am grateful to Galina Aksyonova for making this point.
45    I thank an anonymous reader for noting that this is surely Marguerite Gauthier, 'la Dame aux Camélias'.
46    Not coincidentally, near the end of the film Lilia recalls 'that song about diamonds being a girl's best friend'.
47    P. Kuz'menko, 'Kira Muratova zasypaet i prosypaetsia s mysl'iu o zhivoderne', *Novaia ezhenedel'naia gazeta*, 20 October 1994, p.7.
48    Plakhov, 'Legkaia muza', p.3.
49    Bykov, 'Ia ne koshka', p.50.
50    Plakhov, '*Uvlechen'ia* Muratovoi stanoviatsia vse bolee nevinnymi', *Kommersant*, 5 March 1994.
51    A. Kulish, 'Interesnaia chudachka', *Nezavisimaia gazeta*, 13 March 1994.
52    P. Cherniaev, 'Chut' pomedlennee, koni!', *Prezident*, 23–25 March 1994.
53    V. Turovskii, 'Spasibo za loshadei!', *Izvestiia*, 24 March 1994.
54    Bozhovich, 'Sindrom, no optimisticheskii', *Kul'tura*, 26 March 1994.
55    Bykov, 'Razvlechen'ia liubimoi', *Literaturnaia gazeta*, 6 April 1994.
56    Plakhov, 'Legkaia muza', I. Mantsov, 'Kollektivnoe telo kak romanticheskii geroi-liubovnik', *Iskusstvo kino*, no. 8, 1994, pp.3–13.
57    Bykov, 'Ia ne koshka'.

## Chapter 6

1    J. Knox-Voina, V. Voina, 'Kira Muratova: Mne vsegda khotelos' sdelat' tikhii, skromnyi, normal'nyi fil'm', *Iskusstvo kino*, no. 11, 1997, p.59.
2    The titles credit the following funding sources: the production company of Igor Tolstunov, NTV-Profit, with the participation of Roskomkino, the television company NTV, the Ministry of Art and Culture of Ukraine, the Odessa Studio and Sudzi-fil'm.
3    T. Pozniak, 'Korotkaia vstrecha s Kiroi Muratovoi', *Obshchaia gazeta*, no. 27, 6 July 2000.
4    I. Rubanova, 'Ty, Motsart…', *Iskusstvo kino*, no. 9, 1997 p.93.
5    J. Meek, 'Art Takes Back Seat in Russian Cinema', *The Scotsman*, 25 February 1999.
6    Which was, in turn, based on an early song (op. 7, no. 8) set to the poem by Matthias Claudias (1740–1815). I am indebted to my colleague Christian Rogowski for providing this information.
7    V. Turovskii, 'Vse liudi – urody', *Izvestiia*, 14 January 1997.
8    I. Gladil'shchikov, 'Ubivtsy', *Itogi*, 4 February 1997, p.5.
9    Kharms' narrator is unexpectedly saved by a very Russian deus ex machina: the suitcase is stolen while he is in the toilet on the train.
10    There is a subtext here to yet another Russian classic, Nikolai Gogol', noted by Arkhangelskii, in 'Tema i rema', *Iskusstvo kino*, no. 6, 1997, pp.19–26. The hero of his story 'Vii' has to sit up all night guarding the body of a beautiful witch.
11    Given the context, his opening words – 'Here I am!' (*Vot – eto ia!*) – may also hint at the title of Eduard Limonov's novel of sexual exploits in America, *It's Me, Eddie* [Eto ia – Edichka, 1979].
12    'Ofelia, bezvinno utonuvshaia', *Kinostsenarii*, no. 5, 1994, pp.126–133.

13   E. Plakhova, 'Muratova i Madonna', *Iskusstvo kino*, no. 9, 1997, p.97. She also contrasts the film to *Fargo*: 'The Coens oppose the cynicism and decadence of the lumpens to the soul of the "Corn Belt" ... but in Muratova no one even tries to solve the crime or draw a moral.'

14   A. Bossart, 'Priroda no. 6, ili grecheskii khor Odesskikh koshek', *Vecherniaia Moskva*, 18 February 1997.

15   For a reproduction of Eisenstein's analysis of the shot, see R. Taylor, *The Battleship Potemkin*, London and New York, 2000, pp.36–37.

16   Anna Karenina carried a red purse, mentioned several times by Tolstoy, on her final journey to death under the train. Liza Knapp discusses the symbolic associations that have been attributed to it, adding her own. 'Tolstoy seems to be indicting Anna for having made her other red bag (her sexual/reproductive chambers) into the "container of her desires" and "the bag of her pleasures" rather than into a womb.' 'The Estates of Pokrovskoe and Vozdvizhenskoe: Tolstoy's Labyrinth of Linkings in Anna Karenina', Tolstoy Studies, 1995–1996, no. 8, p.91. Given the importance of Tolstoy for Muratova and the proximity of this episode to the shots of the Greek spiral, I suspect that the attention she pays to Ofa's red purse may link it to Anna's and to its possible sexual symbolism.

17   Gladil'shchikov, 'Ubivtsy'.

18   The Latin name of her superior, Albina, reiterates the white archaic symbolism of the novella.

19   N. Svirilia, 'Chelovek-zver' i chelovek muliazh', *Seans*, no. 15, 1997, p.22.

20   Litvinova's screenplay, like Shakespeare's original, specified a river as the site of Ophelia's drowning, but there are no rivers in Odessa, and Muratova made do with what she had at hand.

21   A. Rutkovskii, 'Nol' za tsivilizatsiiu', *Iskusstvo kino*, no. 9, 1997, p.100.

22   Private conversation, Amherst, MA, April 2003.

23   Inna Broude typifies the complaints of more traditional Russian film critics. 'I don't hear an authorial "voice" in *Three Stories*. This despite the fact that this is, in all respects, an "auteur" film, and Muratova shows us a superlative, cinematically brilliant film.' *Takoe vot kino: russkie fil'my 1990–x*, Tenafly, NJ, 2001, p.106.

24   Arkhangelskii, 'Tema', p.26.

25   A. Koroleva, 'Tri evropeiskie istorii', *Seans*, no.15, 1997, p.23.

26   O. Tabakov, *Moia nastoiashchaia zhizn'*, Moscow, 2000, pp.483–484.

27   Gromov (ed.), *Kira Muratova '98*, pp.76–77.

28   Bossart, 'Priroda'.

29   Arkhangelskii, 'Tema', p.21.

30   *Seans*, no.15, 1997, pp.20–23.

31   Rubanova, 'Ty, Motsart...', p.93.

32   V. Erofeev, 'Proshchanie s gumanizmom', *Iskusstvo kino*, no. 9, 1997, p.95.

33   N. Tsirkun, 'Gorlo bredit britvoiu...' *Iskusstvo kino*, no. 9, 1997, p.98.

34   O. Aronson, 'Mezhdu priomom i attraktsionom', *Iskusstvo kino*, no. 9, 1997, pp.104–105.

35   Plakhov, 'Mne nuzhna'.

## Chapter 7

1   I. Kaprinos, 'A nu, druzhok, na pososhok!', *Kievskie vedomosti*, 4 November 1999, p.12.

2   N. Zorkaia et al., 'Kira Muratova: Liubliu nazyvat' veshchi svoimi imenami', *Iskusstvo kino*, no. 11, 1999, p.82.

3   The film has two official titles: the Russian, written in Cyrillic, and the Ukrainian, written in Latin letters. Both translate identically into English.

4   E. Stishova, 'Poznavaia belyi svet', *Iskusstvo kino*, no. 11, 1999, pp.87–89.

5   Zorkaia et al., 'Liubliu', p.80.

6   I thank Jenny Kallick for identifying the two operatic excerpts on the sound-track. The first, sung during a music lesson Oleg overhears in the stairway, is from Rossini's *Barber of Seville*, Act 1, in which Rosina, with delight, describes her imagined misbehaviour: 'I'll be a viper.' There is, of course, an ironic connection to Lena's behaviour. The final excerpt, from Mimi's aria in Act 1 of *La Bohème*, contains the lines, 'The first sunlight is mine' and 'April's first kiss is mine'.

7   Zorkaia et al., 'Liubliu', p.81.

8   I am grateful to Inna Babyonysheva for calling my attention to it.

9   There is an excellent bilingual edition: Joseph Brodsky, *Nativity Poems*, New York, 2001.

10   N. Shiverskaia, 'Kira Muratova: Zhivye liudi – eto opasno', *Vremia novostei*, 6 June 2001 (www.rol.ru/news/art/kino/01/01/06_004.htm).

11   Sergei Trimbach points to the former subtext in 'V kompanii s idiotami', *Kinoforum*, no. 1, 2002, pp.22–24; Zorkaia prefers the latter in 'Pershoriadni *Drugoriadni liudi*', *Kino-kolo*, no. 10, summer 2001, pp.32–33. In Berlin and Wiesbaden the title was translated as 'Second-class Citizens'. When Zorkaia asked Muratova to explain the wording of the title, she demurred, saying: 'Let it remain a puzzle to you.'

12   Bykov, 'Budet zhit', *Iskusstvo kino*, no. 6, 2001, p.33. He adds, 'In general, aesthetic compliments to a director like Muratova are already banality. It's like praising Lev Tolstoy for his style.'

13   Zorkaia, 'Pershoriadni *Drugoriadni liudi*', *Kino-kolo*, no. 10, summer 2001, p.33.

14   Muratova used a collection of friends and non-professionals, including her husband, for this sequence. M. Gudyma, *Zerkalo nedeli*, 7 November 2000, p.15.

15   Gromov (ed.), *Kira Muratova '98*, p.68.

16   Khvastov, who wears an SS uniform for his cameo role, is a fashion designer and the costume designer for the film.

17   The situation recalls that of Krishtofovich's *A Friend of the Deceased*, in which the depressed hero takes out a contract on himself, but is forced to kill the killer when he finds he can't cancel the contract after he has a change of heart.

18   Trimbach sees in this a nod to the work of Peter Greenaway.

19   Trimbach, 'V kompanii'.

20   O. Koniukh, 'Primkhi doli, abo na zakhist Kiri Muratovovoi', *Kino-kolo* (Kiev), no. 14, summer 2002, pp.16–17.

21   V. Belopolskaia, 'Rezhiser srednykh let na rol' Dostoevskogo', *Russkii zhurnal*, 3 April 2001 (www.russ.ru/culture/review/20010403_blop.html).

22   Bykov, 'Budet zhit', p.32.

23   Zorkaia, 'Pershoriadni', pp.32–33.

24   E. Tarkhanova, 'Chrezvychaino mnogo dobra: 15 minut s Kiroi Georgievnoi Muratovoi', *MK Bul'var*, no. 29, 15 July 2002.
25   A. Dolin, 'Mertvetsy nevozmozhny', 15 April 2002 (www.gzt.ru/rubricator.gzt? rubric=reviu&id=12050000000003015).
26   V. Kichin, 'Marsh entuziastov, postsovetskaia versiia: *Vtorostepennye liudi* Kiry Muratovoi v Moskve', *Izvestiia*, 15 May 2002.
27   Rutkovskii, 'Tetushka Charli', *Nezavisimaia gazeta*, 16 May 2002.
28   E. Pliashkevich, 'Vtorostepennye maski', *Utro. Ezhedenedel'naia elektronnaia gazeta*, www.utro.ru/articles/print/2002052000220578862.shtml.
29   Trimbach, 'V kompanii'.
30   E. Leonova, 'Tantsuiushchie i poiushchie' (www.film.ru/article.asp?ID=3400). See two other reviews of the film at the same site: E. Barabash, 'Vtorostepennyi sindrom' (ID=3401), and K. Tarkhanova, 'Odesskaia gumanitarnaia pomoshch'' (ID=3402).
31   E. Tarkhanova, '…Chrezvychaino'.
32   D. Desiaterik, 'Kira Muratova: V pervuiu ochered' ia khochu nravit'sia sebe samoi', *Den'* (Kiev), no. 137, 1 August 2002, p.5.
33   Plakhov, 'Mne nuzhna lozhka degtia', *Kommersant*, 4 November 1998, p.10.
34   Bykov, 'Nauchila'.
35   Desiaterik, 'V pervuiu'.
36   A.P. Chekhov, *Polnoe sobranie sochinenii i pisem*, vol. 13, Moscow, 1978, p.365.
37   Desiaterik, 'V pervuiu'.
38   Dolin, 'Kira Muratova: Obozhaiu klounadu', *Gazeta.ru*, no. 128, 28 June 2002.
39   'Chekhovskie motivy', screenplay by Kira Muratova with the participation of Evgeni Golubenko. *Kinostsenarii*, no. 1, 2003, p.31.
40   A. Kurina, 'Kira Muratova pislia *Chekhov'skikh motiviv*', *Kino-kolo*, no. 15, August 2000.
41   'From the beginning we wanted a little boy to whom we could simply say, "Sleep!" and he would sleep, or at least pretend. At the same time we wanted him to be very small. An insoluble problem. Finally we gave up – if it won't work out, so what. And suddenly, right in the middle of a take, the actress who was playing his mother said in a whisper: "Look!" We quickly began filming him, and I ordered the actors to continue the conversation. And he kept sleeping. It was a gift.' Desiaterik, 'V pervuiu'.
42   Shooting script.
43   Dolin, 'Obozhaiu'. In one shot of the choir there is a short, dark-haired lady in glasses who looks remarkably like Muratova herself.
44   Dolin, 'Obozhaiu'.
45   Abdullaeva, 'Tret'estepennye liudi', www.miff.ru/rus/moscow/program/film/ ?pid=1&fid=17.
46   E. Sal'nikova, 'Astenicheskii razmakh: Kira Muratova sniala shevdevr', *Nezavisimaia gazeta*, nos. 127–128, 28 June, 2002.
47   A. Dolin, 'Venchal'noe karaoke', *Gazeta*, 28 June, 2002 (also at www.chekhov-motivy.ru)
48   D. Savel'ev, 'Filip Panov', *Premiere*, March 2002.
49   Abdullaeva, 'Sarai ili magazin?', *Iskusstvo kino*, no. 11, 2002, pp.37–44. The film is available on DVD (with English subtitles) from Ruscico.
50   Dolin, 'Venchal'noe'.
51   E. Belostotskaia, 'Da zravstvuet kino!', *Slovo*, no. 27, 5 July 2002.
52   Abdullaeva, 'Tret'estepennye liudi'.

## Chapter 8

1 Plakhov, '*Uvlechen'ia*' Muratovoi'.
2 *Kira Muratova '98* (Moscow [VGIK], 1999), a collection of interviews and essays by students at VGIK, was published in an extremely small edition and is very difficult to obtain.
3 Bozhovich, 'I make films', pp.18–19.
4 Frodon, 'L'oeuvre mutilée', p.72.
5 Bollag and Ciment, 'Entretien', p.10.
6 Getmanchuk, 'Pravda'.
7 Morozova, 'Fikus'.
8 P. Sirkes, 'Kira Muratova: Iskusstvo rodilos' iz zapretov, styda i strakha', *Iskusstvo kino*, no. 2, 1995, p.90.
9 Sirkes, 'Iskusstvo rodilos'', p.96.
10 Zhenin, 'Zhanne d'Ark', p.14.
11 Sviridova, 'Eto moi narkotik'.
12 Bykov, 'Nauchila'.
13 N. Vlashchenko, 'Kira Muratova: Garmoniia – eto narushenie vsekh zakonov', www.day.kiev.ua/1997/219/cultura/cul 1.htm.
14 Priannik, 'Kira Muratova: Nikakie pravila ulichnogo dvizheniia nado mnoi ne vlastny', *Moskovskii komsomolets*, 8 May 1998, p.11.
15 N. Martsuk, 'Kira Muratova: I scrape off the calluses so that at last I can anoint it with oil', http://day.Kiev.ua/Digest/1998/33/culture/.
16 Muratova interview, 1991.
17 Bykov, 'Nauchila'.
18 Zhenin, 'Zhanne d'Ark'.
19 'Iskusstvo – eto utekha, otrada, i opium', *Iskusstvo kino*, no. 7, 1992, p.13.
20 Sviridova, 'Eto moi narkotik'.
21 Gromov (ed.), *Kira Muratova '98*, p.70.
22 Plakhov, 'Kira Muratova: Ia takoi zh narod, kak i drugie', *Seans*, no. 12, 1996, p.168.
23 Priannik, 'Nikakie pravila'.
24 Gromov (ed.), *Kira Muratova '98*, p.65.
25 N. Okhotin, 'Konstatatsiia otchaiania: interv'iu s Kiroi Muratovoi', *Polit.ru*, 13 August 1999 (www.polit.ru/documents/107113.html).
26 Plakhov, 'Ia takoi narod'.
27 Vlashchenko, 'Garmoniia'.
28 Getmanchuk, 'Pravda'.
29 Zhenin, 'Zhanne d'Ark'.
30 Bykov, 'Nauchila'.
31 S. Khoriakova, 'Kira Muratova: Ia - zdorovyi organizm s optimisticheskim ustroistvom', *Kul'tura*, 11 September 1997.
32 Khoriakova, 'Ia - zdorovyi'.
33 Priannik, 'Nikakie pravila'.
34 Zhenin, 'Zhanne d'Ark'.
35 Khoriakova, 'Ia - zdorovyi'.
36 Vlashchenko, 'Garmoniia'.
37 Gromov (ed.), *Kira Muratova '98*, pp.67–68.
38 Gromov (ed.), *Kira Muratova '98*, p.79.

39  Khoriakova, 'Ia – zdorovyi'.
40  Priannik, 'Nikakie pravila'. Muratova's daughter, Marianna, died in 2000, leaving her to raise two teenage grandsons.
41  Martsuk, 'Kira Muratova: I scrape off the calluses so that at last I can anoint it with oil'.
42  Gromov (ed.), *Kira Muratova '98*, p.69.
43  Gromov (ed.), *Kira Muratova '98*, pp.72–73.
44  Gromov (ed.), *Kira Muratova '98*, pp.73–74.
45  Okhotin, 'Konstatatsiia otchaianiia'.
46  H.-J. Schlegel, 'Befreiende Schock-therapien: Eine Laudatio auf Kira Muratova', *Berliner Kunstpreis 1999*, Akademie der Künste Berlin, 1999, pp.5–10. I am grateful to Dr Schlegel for providing me with a copy. A slightly abridged Russian translation was published in *Ekran i stsena*, nos. 19–20, May 1999, p.10.
47  O. Novikova, 'Berlins'ki zustrichi z Kiroiu Muratovoiu ta Andzheem Vaidoiu', *Kino-Teatr* (Kiev), no. 3, 2000, p.37.

# Filmography

*By the Steep Ravine* [U krutogo iara, 1961]

*Our Honest Bread* [Nash chestnyi khleb, 1964]

*Brief Encounters* [Korotkie vstrechi, 1967]

*The Long Farewell* [Dolgie provody, 1971]

*Getting to Know the Big, Wide World* [Poznavaia belyi svet, 1978]

*Among the Grey Stones* [Sredi serykh kamnei, 1983]

*A Change of Fate* [Peremena uchasti, 1987]

*Asthenic Syndrome* [Astenicheskii sindrom, 1989]

*The Sentimental Policeman* [Chuvstvitel'nyi militsioner, France/Ukraine, 1992]

*Enthusiasms* [Uvlechen'ia, Russia, 1994]

*Three Stories* [Tri istorii, Russia/Ukraine, 1997]

*Letter to America* (short) [Pis'mo v Ameriku/List do Ameriky, Ukraine, 1999]

*Minor People* [Vtorostepennye liudi, Ukraine, 2001]

*Chekhov's Motifs* [Chekhovskie motivy, Russia/Ukraine, 2002]

*The Tuner* [Nastroishchik, Russia/Ukraine, 2004]